The Bible Study Group:
An Owner's Manual

William Riley

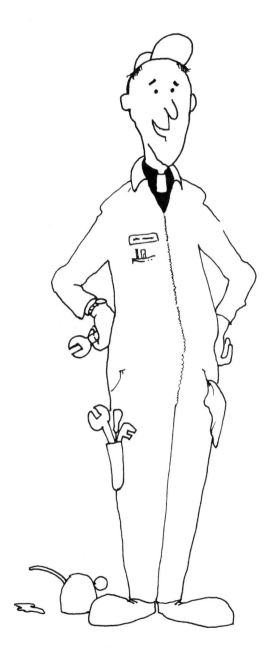

The Bible Study Group:

An Owner's Manual

Drawings by Theo Payne

Ave Maria Press
Notre Dame, Indiana

First published, 1983, by Veritas Publications,
7/8 Lower Abbey Street, Dublin 1, Ireland.

Imprimatur:
† Joseph Carroll
Dublin Diocesan Administrator
December 30, 1984

Library of Congress Catalog Card Number: 85-70362
International Standard Book Number: 0-87793-286-7

Design: Liam Miller
Illustrations: Theo Payne

Printed and bound in the United States of America.

Contents

Introduction

Welcome to the adventures of group Bible study! Whether you are an avid reader of Scripture yourself or a person more aware of the limitations than of the scope of your biblical knowledge, you are about to add a new dimension to your experience of the Word of God as soon as you set up the first meeting of your Bible group. Because most of Scripture was written to be heard by groups rather than isolated individuals, the Bible finds itself at home when a group is studying it.

This book is intended to give some help in the setting up of such a study group and in the work of the group for the first year. The shorter first part of the book deals with some of the mechanics of a Bible group, written for the person who is contemplating beginning a group for the first time. The leader whose group has developed a few engine problems might find some explanation and useful advice in Part One. The leader of a group which is operating smoothly might prefer to move directly to Part Two.

Part Two is by far the more important section of the book; it gives material for twenty-two study sessions which open the Scriptures to the group according to a definite plan of attack. Even though these sessions were primarily intended for groups beginning their exploration of the Word of God, they have also been used successfully by groups with two or three years of Bible study behind them.

Books, unfortunately, do not drop fully formed from the carriage of an author's typewriter. Many thanks are due to all who have helped in the production of this volume, either by the time and effort which they themselves have invested or by their suggestions and encouragements. I also wish to express my gratitude to those who have shared their visions and insights into Scripture with me over the years, as well as those who have allowed me to share mine with them. If this book is of any use to you, then know that it is such people as these that have made it possible.

Part One

The Mechanics of a
Bible Study Group

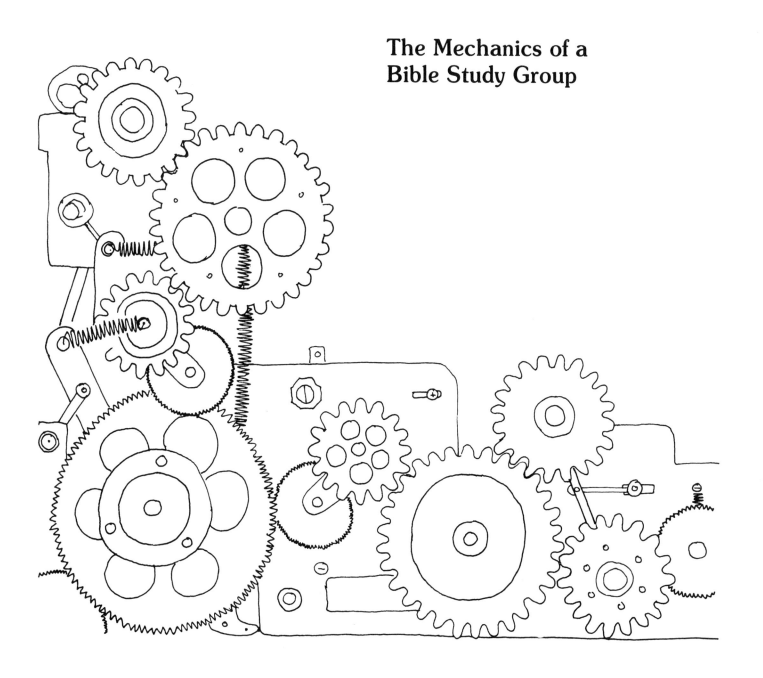

1 A Famine in the Land

Simon Peter found himself a patch of shade from the Palestine sun and sat down. "They have a point," he grudgingly admitted to himself.

Representatives of the Greek speaking Christians had been to see him. Simon wasn't a leader long enough to realise that deputations meant trouble. They had complained that when the food was handed out to needy Christian widows it was a case of Hebrew speakers first and Greek speakers for the leftovers.

No one had planned it that way. No one had planned it at all. Someone had said, "Wouldn't it be a good idea if we pooled a bit of food for the widows?" And that's just what they did. But as the Church grew, so did the number of widows. Sometimes there was plenty for everyone, but sometimes there wasn't and someone was left short. And then there were complaints. And now the Greek speakers felt that they were always at the end of the queue. Things were much simpler before Pentecost, when the whole Church could fit into one room.

"To do this thing properly will mean a lot of work," Peter mused. "First thing is a list of widows, find out exactly how many we have. Then we can figure out how much each able-bodied Christian should contribute to the fund. Then we have to take into account how many can only give now and again and who can afford to give more. Then we have to sort the food and supervise the distribution. Then, please God, everything would be done fairly and there would be no complaints. After all, we can't have people going hungry."

Even this bit of planning was beginning to give Simon a headache. Twenty-five years of throwing a fishing net into the Sea of Galilee didn't necessarily give you organisational aptitude. "Levi is the man for the job, with his expertise in drawing up scales of taxes and all." Peter was relieved to find a suitable scapegoat. But another troubling thought hit Simon Peter from behind when he wasn't looking: was it right to saddle any one of the Twelve with the job of quartermaster? Was this the reason that Jesus had said to them, "Follow me"? Half of Jerusalem still hadn't really heard about Jesus, and

Giving up the service of the word to wait on tables?

even the surrounding countryside was next to untouched by the news of Jesus' death and resurrection. And here was himself, leader of the followers of Jesus, slowing down the work by apportioning off some of his limited manpower before the work had even really begun.

Simon's mind was made up. He returned to the community later that day to announce his decision.

"It wouldn't be right for any of the Twelve to abandon the Word of God to go around serving at tables! You'd best pick out a few outstanding people from yourselves and we'll hand this whole affair over to them. But we have to busy ourselves with prayer and the work of the Word of God" (Cf. Acts 6:1-4.).

"Well, goodnight and safe home. I'll give that matter some thought and get in touch with you soon." Father Simon Peterson waved goodbye, closed the hall door and turned out the front light.

"People must think that the clergy have nothing to do," he thought, half-angry, half self-pitying. Another group of parishioners had called with "a little favour to ask, Father". They wanted him to start a Bible study group in the parish. And from their enthusiasm you could tell that they had expected a "Yes" on the spot! You never knew what a ring at the front bell would mean when you lived in a priest's house.

Lacking any other friend to turn to, Fr Peterson took out his pocket diary to console him. "Just take this week for example," he raged to himself, "Monday night is the finance meeting, and it just wouldn't do to miss that. Tuesday night is the parish bingo — they nearly expect me to come back off my holidays to call out the numbers. Wednesday night I meet with the school board of management. Thursday night I'm at the St Vincent de Paul conference. Saturday night means confessions and Sunday is the evening Mass."

He passed over Friday night in silence, since that was the clerical poker night. Even when speaking to himself, he felt that to bring it up would only be distracting.

"The days are as bad", he continued. "Between schools and hospital and visiting the sick and counselling sessions and managing the plant and the hundred-and-one other things that come up every day, I'm surprised that I get the time to prepare my Sunday homily, let alone prepare a Bible study session."

Half of Fr Peterson's congregation would have been surprised to think that Fr Peterson's Sunday homilies were prepared at all.

On the whole he was well used to dealing with people's requests. When the people came to set up a parish bridge club, he had organised an unused room in the school. When some of the teenagers wanted an old person's flat to paint and wallpaper, he supplied them with ten worthy candidates. He was even good at pouring cold water on the less reasonable requests. Would he ever forget the time that Jack Cauldwell wanted a private audience with the Pope arranged for during his three day visit to Rome? Luckily the pontiff was due to be in Africa at that time, so the matter was quickly solved. Otherwise there might have been some hurt feelings over not being given a cup of tea from the papal china; Jack was the touchy type, and you never knew how he would take things.

All of Fr Peterson's skills had failed him tonight, however. He could think of no real answer, no real excuse. All he did was sit there and listen to them — this group of enthusiasts — until they had run out of things to say (which was a tortuous fifteen minutes), and then that pathetic seeing them to the door and promise to think it over.

And that's what had him so angry. Why couldn't he think of the dozen good reasons that their request was unreasonable? Why couldn't he have told them of all the demands on his time? Why didn't he say to them that he already had a list of unstarted projects as long as your arm and each one as worthy as the next?

Why didn't he believe his own arguments when there wasn't even someone arguing against him?

"Alright. They have a point", he grudgingly admitted to himself. "If they want to study the Bible then they have a right to encouragement. Besides, where else do I send them? To do a correspondence course? To spend three years at the theological faculty of a seminary? But what do they expect from me?"

It was too late to get involved in much of anything that night, so Fr Peterson slumped down in a very comfortable armchair in front of a very boring television newscaster. His mind went back to that haunting request. He shifted in the chair, but it was no use. He definitely heard the weatherman say that there was a dangerous Bible group forming in the east and moving towards the south during the night. Fr Peterson reached for the 'phone and dialled.

"Hello, Jacinta? Fr Simon, here. . . . Yes, I've thought it over, although I haven't really got it worked out yet. What I really wanted to know was, do you think that Tuesday night would suit the others to drop round and discuss this whole thing a bit more?"

Those two situations have a lot in common: people experience a need which they feel the leaders of the Church should fill. In the first case, the need was for food; in the second, for the Word of God. In both cases people were hungry.

In the modern scenario, hunger might not be the right word; I would prefer "undernourished". Perhaps even "undernourished and overfed". People are turning to many places to fill their spiritual hunger: Eastern religious ideas repackaged for the mass market appeal, the mass media pumping out the shallow gospel of consumerism, all the answers to life crammed into a hundred-and-sixteen pages of a bestseller on pop-psychology or pop-philosophy or pop-medicine. People are starving, and they stuff themselves with spiritual junk-food! Overfed, maybe, but certainly undernourished.

At least the ten-year-old girl who gorges herself with chocolates on Christmas night has had the opportunity of a decent Christmas dinner earlier in the day. What alternative do people have for their spiritual junk-food? Is the religious training of their childhood enough to last them a lifetime? Is the five to ten minute Sunday homily really enough to chew on for a week? For many it has already lost its flavour before the Sunday liturgy is finished and — like chewing gum which has likewise shown its limitations — is left behind them as they exit from the pew. People should be offered more nourishment than that.

Christians have never dismissed lightly the need to feed the hungry; the incident about the distribution of food to the widows referred to before proves that. But Christians have seen as even more important this spiritual feeding of the Word of God, as that same incident shows. And Paul's letters back up that picture. His job as a minister of Christ is to preach and teach the gospel, and even the sacraments take a second place to that task (I Cor 1:17; see also Rms 15:16 and Col 4:3-4). Even in the darkest ages of the Church, the message of the Scriptures was given to people in many ways: stained-glass windows and sculptured crosses, picture Bibles for the unlettered and mystery plays to tell the stories of the Bible in the language which people would understand.

Unfortunately, in more modern times, the Bible was not thought of as a book for ordinary Catholics. Robert Browning's mischievous *Soliloquy of the Spanish Cloister* probably summed up the attitude of many a good Catholic in the pew about the reading of Scripture on one's own:

> *There's a great text in Galatians,*
> *Once you trip on it, entails*
> *Twenty-nine distinct damnations,*
> *One sure, if another fails.*

Yes, the private reading of Scripture could be dangerous, thought the Catholic of the Victorian era. It's something that Protestants do. If you have a Bible (purely for keeping family records in, understand) then keep it where no one will actually read it.

Yet at the end of the same century that Browning wrote those verses, Pope Leo XIII wrote an encyclical on the study of Scripture, *Providentissimus Deus*. A single quotation will serve to show in what high regard that pontiff held the necessity of reading the Bible:

> It is right for Jerome to assert that "Ignorance of the Scriptures is ignorance of Christ". He certainly stands out from these writings, as if they were his living and breathing image. From there the ease of afflictions, the encouragement to virtue, the invitation to divine love is extended, marvellous and clear. Certainly what applied to the Church — her institution, nature, her duties and her gifts — so often do they occur by mention there and so many and so ready and strong are the arguments for her that the same Jerome declared most truly: "The person strengthened by the witnesses of Sacred Scripture is a veritable bulwark of the Church."

Despite words like these, echoed by Pope Benedict XV in *Spiritus Paraclitus* (1920) and Pius XII in *Divino Afflante*

Spiritu (1943), the lay Catholic often believed that the teaching Church did not want him to read the Bible. Such a myth had to be exploded by the Second Vatican Council; its whole inspiration and goal seemed to be the Sacred Scriptures. The subsequent synods of bishops, too, have shown special concern with getting the Bible known — especially the synods on evangelisation and catechesis. See, for example, how central the Word of God is in the very concept of catechesis:

> Catechesis aims therefore at developing understanding of the mystery of Christ in the light of God's Word, so that the whole of a person's humanity is impregnated by that Word (*Catechesi Tradendae* §20).

This document, which Pope John Paul II composed in light of the deliberations of the 1977 Synod of Bishops, has a special application to the subject of this book. We presumably are talking about the needs of those who have heard and accepted the basic message of Jesus Christ; the concern of catechesis is the building up and enriching of the faith already received:

> To put it more precisely: within the whole process of evangelisation, the aim of catechesis is to be the teaching and maturation stage, that is to say, the period in which the Christian, having accepted by faith the person of Jesus Christ as the one Lord and having given him complete adherence by sincere conversion of heart, endeavours to know better this Jesus to whom he has entrusted himself: to know his "mystery", the Kingdom of God proclaimed by him, the requirements and promises contained in his Gospel message, and the paths that he has laid down for any one who wishes to follow him.
>
> It is true that being a Christian means saying "yes" to Jesus Christ, but let us remember that this "yes" has two levels: it consists in surrendering to the Word of God and relying on it, but it also means, at a later stage, endeavouring to know better and better the profound meaning of this Word (*Catechesi Tradendae* §20).

Catechetics, however, remains largely the religious instruction of children for most of us. Perhaps the Word is too reminiscent of "catechism", a term associated with our own school days. Finishing the catechism gave a certain sense of accomplishment, as if all the revealed truths of God were now safely packed away in the subconscious for later reference. What need could there possibly be for further enlightenment on matters religious?

> I cannot fail to emphasise now one of the most constant concerns of the Synod Fathers, a concern imposed with vigour and urgency by present experiences throughout the world: I am referring to the central problem of the catechesis of adults. This is the principal form of catechesis, because it is addressed to persons who have the greatest responsibilities and the capacity to live the Christians' message in its fully developed form. The Christian community cannot carry out a permanent catechesis without the direct and skilled participation of adults, whether as receivers or as promoters of catechetical activity. The world in which the young are called to live and give witness to the faith which catechesis seeks to deepen and strengthen is governed by adults: the faith of these adults too should continually be enlightened, stimulated and renewed, so that it may pervade the temporal realities in their charge. Thus, for catechesis to be effective, it must be permanent, and it would be quite useless if it stopped short just at the threshold of maturity, since catechesis, admittedly under another form, proves no less necessary for adults (*Catechesi Tradendae* §43).

"This is the principal form of catechesis. . ." It may be the principal form, but for most of our local churches it is far from the commonest form. We pour our energies and resources into the classrooms, yet after our people leave the school building behind them, they also leave all opportunities for instruction and enrichment of their faith. While no one would deny that religious instruction in school is vital, further religious education for adults is not even a possibility for a large number of Catholics in our society.

We can even find ourselves in the ridiculous situation of concentrating our energies in educating those who aren't particularly keen on being educated (itself a necessary risk) while ignoring those who are crying out for it. Once I was introduced to a teacher, as myself lecturing in Scripture in a college of education. He asked me did I know such-and-such a scholar who had given a marvellous course on Luke's Gospel last year, or a different scholar who had given two days of lectures on a different biblical subject somewhere else. I knew them both, and was pleased that he had found their courses so interesting and stimulating. Keeping the conversation going, I enquired who had been his own lecturer in Scripture during his not-so-distant days of training. "Oh, I can't really remember. You see, back then I wasn't interested." At least for him, thankfully, there was someone to spread the table when he realised that he was hungry.

But are others so fortunate? That Bible which we realise more than ever is so central to our faith remains a closed book to many committed Catholics. How can they gain access to it? Most of the many books written as an introduction to the Bible presume some kind of theological background before you start. Besides, learning to read the Bible from a book can be about as fruitful as learning to dance from an essay on the waltz. It is something that you learn from doing and from someone who will show you how.

I'm not sure if Fr Peterson ever solved his dilemma. His goodwill and pastoral commitment probably led him to make the right decision. If he is still pondering, if he can't make up his mind, maybe a final quotation from that document on catechesis would help him:

> For your part, priests, here you have a field in which you are the immediate assistants of your bishops. The Council has called you "instructors in the faith"; there is no better way for you to be such instructors than by devoting your best efforts to the growth of your communities in the faith. Whether you are in charge of a parish, or are chaplains to primary or secondary schools or universities, or have responsibility for pastoral activity at any level, or are leaders of large or small communities, especially youth groups, the Church expects you to neglect nothing with a view to a well-organised and well-oriented catechetical effort. . . All believers have a right to catechesis; all pastors have the duty to provide it. . . With all my strength, I beg you, ministers of Jesus Christ, do not, for lack of zeal or because of some unfortunate preconceived idea, leave the faithful without catechesis. Let it not be said that "the children beg for food, but no one gives it to them" (*Catechesi Tradendae* §64).

2 Who Should lead?

The chances are if you have bought this book and have made it this far in reading it, that you are contemplating getting a Bible group together. The chances also are — unless you have someone definite in mind who would take charge of such a group — that you will end up as group leader. Now don't panic. Let's discuss this thing like adults and look at what is expected from the leader of a Bible group.

You may have your own ideas. You may think that a Bible group leader should be a person trained in Greek and Hebrew to the extent that they pray in those tongues, who spends every holiday on archaeological digs in Palestine, and who reads the genealogical lists of the Old Testament for light entertainment. This person, too, is an expert communicator who has a precise answer for any question which might be asked, who would never dream of starting a session without slide projector, filmstrips, tapes and printed handouts all prepared beforehand. In your heart of hearts you know that when the three-hour session comes to an end, the over-crowded hall of biblical enthusiasts breaks out into applause and begs for just one more hour. Put your mind at rest. There is no such leader, and that sort of charisma will hardly be required of you.

The first qualification of the study group leader is educational; but because that term might conjure up notions of post-graduate degrees and the like, I would prefer to look at this requirement as one of *understanding*. No one comes to a Bible group to examine the leader's pieces of paper or to count the number of letters after his name. People come to learn to understand the Scriptures and their faith, and to share the understanding and insights of the group leader.

The group leader will naturally want a good understanding of the Bible, but that doesn't mean a detailed knowledge of it. The type of understanding which is essential for starting off is what Scripture is and what Scripture is for. Don't worry if you can't say right off how many books are in the New Testament — you can always turn to the title page and count them. But if you don't have a clue about what makes this Volume different from all of the other written works which humanity has produced, then we have problems.

The *purpose* of Scripture is the first thing to be clear about. The Bible has been misused in many ways: to start eccentric cults and new religions, to hammer suspected heretics, to prove that members of other races aren't fully human, and probably even to prop up a short leg on the kitchen table. The purpose of Scripture is something quite different: it is there to lead us to God. It is not there to give us ancient statistics or to prove the theory of evolution wrong. It was written to show us why we live, how to live, and for whom to live; it is the unfolding of God's great plan for humanity.

But there is no real understanding of the Bible without some understanding of its *conditionings*. The Scriptures are not just the Word of God, they are also words of men. They were not written in our language or our culture, and the better we are disposed to seeing the differences, the better we will understand the Scriptures themselves. The person who begins to read the Scriptures with an immutable conviction that *every* word of the Bible is written to fit his own cultural and philosophical specification, who thinks that everything must be literally accurate in the Word of God to be true, has amputated a leg before he has even begun the race. The good group leader will understand how important it is to place any scriptural passage against its background if its beauty and truth are to be appreciated.

But if the Bible's role for the Christian isn't understood, then it doesn't make sense to lead a Bible group at all. Unless the leader knows that Scripture is a treasury — and one that the leader himself or herself has far from exhausted — the Scripture group could well degenerate into a lifeless intellectual exercise. The leader should allow the Scriptures to interact with the members of the group — to challenge, to prod, to comfort, to encourage, to entertain, to shock and to edify.

There are other types of understanding which the group leader needs as well. Some general understanding of theology and the central doctrines of the Church are required, since the Bible does not exist in a vacuum but is part (a very central part) of a larger world of faith. Church teaching and theology grow out of the revelation of Scripture, are the result of two thousand years of studying and trying to live the Bible; they form the context in which we read the Bible today. Equally important in leading a Bible group is an understanding of where the people who make up the group are in their own approach. The world's greatest expert in the prophecies of Deutero-Zechariah could be a disaster at a session of the parish Bible group, simply because he has no feel for the problems which people have in fleshing out the Word of God with their lives.

Another qualification for the group leader is the ability to communicate. To call that an ability to "teach" would be too limiting. Of course a good teacher will be a good group leader, but that is also true of a good story-teller or a good speaker or even a good conversationalist. The adult Bible group is not a twelve-year-olds' religion class come of age. The abilities and talents of the leader will go a long way in determining its structure, and every social talent which the leader possesses will be an added asset to his or her leadership.

Something desirable, though not essential, is that the leader has some standing with the community from which group members are drawn. This might not be so true of someone who offers evening classes in re-upholstering armchairs, but when the study involves something as basic as one's faith, group members might want to know that the leader is competent to talk about such matters and has some authority to deal with things spiritual.

Remember that picture of the "ideal leader" which we painted at the beginning of the chapter? Perhaps that picture wasn't so ideal after all. If such a leader ever existed, there would be one essential ingredient which might be missing: the group leader must be a fellow learner. The leader must be intent on letting the experience of the Bible group widen his own vision and increase his own understanding. Normally the group leader sees his or her limitations well enough to be open to the learning experience. That growth might occur during the leader's preparation for the meeting, or perhaps through contributions from the floor. The Holy Spirit never gave exclusive rights to his services to the leaders of any Bible study group.

The leader will be asked questions which will make his whole incompetence flash before his eyes.

No potential leader should feel that he must be an expert before the group begins. Although a good leader might seem an expert to many members of the group, he will very rarely be an expert by qualification. At many stages, he will find himself only a couple of chapters "ahead of the posse". He will sometimes be as perplexed by a verse as anyone else at the session. He will be asked questions which will make his whole incompetence flash before his eyes in a second. Yet throughout it all, he can comfort himself with the certain knowledge that — of all of the people in the group — he will be the one who will learn most about the Scripture and who will benefit most from the study. As one self-instruction book put it, "If you want to deepen your knowledge, go through this book again. If you *really* want to learn it, teach it to someone else".

Now that we have outlined the sort of qualities which we are looking for, we can cast a quick glance at some of the candidates for the job.

The priest, we must admit, has everything going for him. He has a background in theology and scriptural study, he has standing in the local church if only by virtue of his office. Not only does he usually have a fair skill at getting things across, he has been using that skill Sunday after Sunday in speaking about the Word of God. His own role in the Liturgy of the Word can only benefit from any effort which he invests in a

17

Bible study group. Leading people in the study of Scripture is part of his job as a minister of the Word. It is a pity that so many priests feel that they do not have the competence to conduct sessions of group Scripture study; the truth is that they are probably the most competent people in the majority of situations. They will fully appreciate their own knowledge and appreciation of the Bible when they begin to share it with others.

Of course there are others who share the work of the ministry of the Word already active in the local community. The trained catechist has the background and the skills, and spent a long time acquiring them. Other teachers, too, often have some training in the study of Scripture and certainly have much expertise in matters of education; they also often have the natural respect of those who might join a local group.

A certain pride of place must go to religious sisters and brothers. Quite often their knowledge of the Word of God runs much deeper than they even admit to themselves. Many of them have received some formal training in Scripture and theology, all of them have spent much time and thought on its texts. Catholics seem to expect those in religious life to be in the vanguard of all Christian education; they haven't disappointed our expectations in matters of adult Scripture study, either.

Sometimes it will happen that one of the rank and file members of the group will have to act as leader. Hopefully that person will have spent some time in Bible study before the group ever formed — but sometimes the chosen leader will be as green as anyone else in the room. In such a case, the group will have to rely heavily on outside aids such as books and tapes. The work is more difficult that way, but it can be done. Even in such conditions it is better to have people studying God's Word than no opportunity at all.

No one can take on the leadership of a group without a certain commitment to preparing the work of the session. Exactly how much time the preparation takes and what sort of work goes into it depends very much on the abilities of the leader and the form that the group takes. A few things will always be part of getting ready for a session, though, no matter who is involved.

The essential is reading the Scriptures. Reading and re-reading and re-reading again. It might seem an aspect nearly too obvious to mention were it not for the fact that it is often more fun to read *about* the Bible than to read the Bible itself. Yet most of what can be said about a passage is to be found in the passage itself and in other related biblical texts. If you have a smattering of the original languages (don't get excited — no one said that you had to have the original languages) then you would be foolish not to cast an eye over the Hebrew or Greek text. If Hebrew and Greek are, well, Greek to you, then use more than one translation when you read. You might be struck by something in a new translation which you have left unnoticed in your favourite version for years. If you know a language besides English, try to read the text in that language as well; something from the Greek which just can't be translated into English might have made it in French or Latin or Swahili. But the main thing is, read the text.

Most of the time, you will want to take a look at the commentaries as well. Remember, though, that the most scholarly commentaries might also prove the ones most useless to yourself and your group. Find commentaries which say something to you and which bring across the sense of the passage to the forefront. But if you find that you are paying more attention to what the commentary says in your preparation than what the text is saying, then you are using the commentary badly. Commentaries should enhance your own reading of the text, not replace it. Never finalise your session preparation immediately after looking at a commentary; go back and read the text again first. If what was in the commentary was useful, it will show in your final reading of the text.

There are other ways of broadening your horizons, of course. If you are a regular reader of religious publications, you will often find in them articles on biblical matters. A wander through a good religious bookshop could put your finances in jeopardy even if you confine yourself to books on Scripture written at your own level. If you have a passing interest in ancient history or geography, not to mention mythology or archaeology, these will all help to enrich your own understanding of the Bible and indirectly benefit your group.

Something nearly as inescapable as reading the text is writing down a few notes. Don't write down everything that you're going to say; you aren't delivering a learned paper to a group of scholars, you're talking about the Word of God to a few interested fellow students. Although the session should be relaxed and informal, you will need reminders of where you are heading, interesting things to point out, cross references to other relevant passages, and so on. Even if you don't as much as look at them during the session itself, writing out the notes will help you to organise the material and to notice any imbalances or omissions you may have otherwise overlooked. And it can be amazingly useful to be able to look up what you had done in a previous session, especially if you are going to talk on the same subject to a different group.

The second part of this book does a good deal of preparation work for you, at least for twenty-two sessions. Each session is introduced by a short essay which gives some bearings on the subject matter for the session. Then there are notes for use during the session itself. These notes are much more lengthy than what I would write out for my own use before a session, but then we're trying to make things easy for you, aren't we? A few comments on selected verses from the passage under study are also supplied. It would be the rare leader who would use everything supplied in the essay and notes during a session and the rare group that would let him. There are so many wonderfully enticing distractions that are bound to sidetrack anyone.

These few pages on what to look for in a group leader and on what is involved in preparing for a session should give you a fair idea of whether you can take on the task or not. Or whether the person you originally had in mind could take on the task or not. Whoever does it is sure to find it rewarding and enriching; those who decline it will never know what they missed.

3 What Type of Group?

Bible groups, like the people who make them up, come in a variety of shapes and sizes. There are energetic ones and ones that are more relaxed; there are the hefty eaters and those who prefer to pick at the fare offered them; there are talkative ones as well as those that are rather shy.

Before ever a meeting of the group takes place, hard decisions have to be made about what type of a group it will be. Those decisions can be altered once the group has formed and started to work together. You might think that it is impossible to make such decisions before you actually see the group itself, but you already have quite a bit of the information you need to hand.

There are basically three factors which will decide your group: the leader, the people who make up the group, and the aims of the group. Hopefully you have some idea of the personality of the leader, especially as we are presuming that it is yourself. The approach of the group must be one in which the leader is at home; if the leader is uncomfortable, everyone will be uncomfortable. The leader should know in what structures his or her abilities to communicate reach their optimum. Within reason, of course; the manager of the local lounge bar may not be willing to lease his premises to a Scripture study group one night a week.

The aim of the group is also something which you will have to determine beforehand, and which will also depend to some degree on the personality of the leader. When people actually start meeting, they will come with many different hopes and expectations. Some will come to deepen their faith; some will come because they have problems with their belief. I actually once had a group member who later told me that she had come to lose her faith: she no longer wanted to be a Christian, but felt that she had not given Christianity enough of an opportunity to explain itself. This was going to be a last-ditch effort, and after that she could happily become an agnostic. She was telling me this, happy that her original intention had been disappointed. Some will come for a bit of mental stimulation, and some just for a night out. The intentions of the various members are usually too widespread across the spectrum to pool together and get a common "aim". The leader should choose an aim for the group broad enough to cater for many of the potential members, and then tailor it as the sessions proceed. Possible aims might be to get an overall view of the Bible, or to look at one particular section with application to everyday living, or perhaps to look at the lectionary readings for the following Sunday. Aims for a Bible group can include intellectual aims as well as spiritual ones and — to a lesser extent — social ones.

The final factor in determining the approach you take is the group itself. Its size can make you alter your plans drastically: if you had planned for a discussion group and seventy-five people turn up, or if you had planned to deliver forty-five minute lectures and two people turn up, you had better be flexible enough to change your structure. Most groups will be a mixture of all types, young and old, educated and not so educated, strongly committed and religiously insecure. But sometimes groups will have a more common background: groups which have a well-defined stratum from which members are invited, for example. Groups like that have been formed for university students or for members of the

Total input from the group

charismatic movement or for retired members of the community. If you know that the group will have some sort of common background before you begin, then you can also take this into consideration when deciding the group's structure.

There are two extremes which are the boundaries of the choices before you at this stage. We could call these *total input from the leader* and *total input from the group*. The first is a straightforward lecture; people come with their notebooks, get up and leave when it's over, and if they say so much as "goodnight" to each other on the way out — well, that's optional. Such an approach has its valid uses, as in a series of public lectures, but it is hardly what we have in mind for our Bible group. The second extreme might also be called *total sharing*, where everyone says what they want to and the leader acts as a kind of timekeeper. This, too, can be disastrous; it might be great for a group therapy session, but it doesn't work for studying the Word of God. If people want to learn about Scripture, there must be some way for information to be communicated — not just a pooling of private opinions. The real possibilities lie somewhere in the vast field between these two extremes.

The first possibility which we will consider is the *guided discussion*. This would be a definite discussion group, but one in which there is a certain input of information. The group itself would have to be reasonably small, and the people in it would have to be willing to do good preparation outside of the group meetings. To really work, the passage under consideration has to be reasonably short, usually under a chapter in length, or else the discussion ranges too far afield. The input, or information to be contributed, must be brief, able to be given in a couple of minutes at the start and perhaps augmented as the discussion evolves. The responsibility for preparing and presenting the input might be revolved around the group week by week, but the leader or chairperson should remain the same. It takes certain skills to be an effective chairperson of such a group, to ensure that the shyer members make their contribution without bullying them and to prevent others from saddling up their hobbyhorses and riding off into the sunset, leaving the rest of the group behind choking in the dust. Such a group has the distinct advantage of being the most informal structure and the best possibility of getting the members to know one another.

We'll call the second approach the *teach-in*. Here the leader has a definite input of information to make, and a considerable input, but it is communicated in a sort of to-ing and fro-ing between himself and the group. He gets the group members to contribute their own observations, experiences and insights and builds on them. Basically the leader is doing the talking, but not to the exclusion of what the group members have to say. The burden of preparation will lie on the leader in this situation, but if the group members are to make their contribution, they too will have had to do some work on the passage before they come to the meeting.

The third possibility is the one which I use myself, although aware of its limitations. It is the *talk with discussion*, where the

Total input from the leader

input is communicated in the form of a twenty to forty minute talk which is followed by a session for questions and discussion. The main advantage is that the maximum amount of information on a text can be given in a session; the main disadvantage is that the contribution of group members can be confined more or less to questions and there is very little interplay between the group members themselves. Then, too, preparing and delivering a talk does not suit every possible leader's style of communication. It is vital to try to make the group members interact, not to allow them to be mere passive isolated listeners... although some members will opt for that no matter what structure the group adopts.

The twenty-two sessions in the second part of the book are written from experience with the *talk and discussion* type of group. It might be an idea, then, to give you some idea of a typical meeting of this sort. Once the members have assembled, the meeting begins with a short prayer, often the Our Father. Then the group members might be asked for insights into the text which they have prepared for the session; sometimes that takes the form of answers to questions which they have worked on during the week. Although questions like that should not be too difficult, they should be broad enough for a few different answers to emerge. After a few minutes of this, the talk is given. It is important that it is not a paper which is read, or an extended homily. Some sort of visual aid helps, even if it is only a piece of chalk and a blackboard, and the talk should be lightened occasionally with the odd funny story, topical aside, or what-have-you. Remember, you are competing with the television and the video-recorder. After the talk, the group members who are still conscious nudge those who have fallen into peaceful slumber and there is a ten-minute break for a cup of tea. This break gives the members a chance to talk with one another informally, at times, hopefully, on the subject matter of the session. In our local group, we had to introduce a rule that no large group discussion emerge at this time — there's plenty of time for that after. After the break, there is a time for questions. Most of these come from the floor on matters arising from the talk or from the reading material;

the leader needs to be vigilant here lest the questions stray onto distant fields. This particular leader has vivid and disturbing memories of a night when one member successfully edged the discussion towards a monologue on the absence of church bells. The leader should also throw some questions back to the floor, especially questions which might have an assortment of possible answers. Then, too, the leader should have a few questions to ask the group; sometimes the questions which have been prepared by the group are saved until this point. Room must be made for questions which the group might want to ask, but there should also be an element of discussion in this part of the session. Don't be too disappointed if some nights, especially in the early days of the group, no real discussion emerges. There will be other nights when you nearly have to bring out the tear gas to bring the discussion to an end. At the end of the question and discussion (and it is no harm to have a set time at which to call a halt — better to have everyone still interested than most of them bored to tears while a few die-hards keep the discussion going), the session ends with a time for prayer. In our group, this is a miniature Liturgy of the Word, but groups will find their own prayer level. More on that in chapter six.

There are many other possible structures for a Bible study group, but most of them fit more or less into one of these three types. There are groups that meet to listen to a tape by a scholar on a biblical topic, and then discuss the subject for that session. This is basically the *talk and discussion* meeting (with the exception that the speaker is not available afterwards to answer questions). There is also the session in which all of the members read some material about the passage as well as the passage itself, and then come together to discuss the matter. My publisher and his bank manager feel that the essays and notes in the second half of this book are admirably suitable for this purpose. Such a group would then become a type of *guided discussion* group.

Two other types of approach deserve a mention: the first is the *prayer and Bible study* group. This is basically a prayer group which uses Scripture extensively. Strictly speaking, we are no longer in the realm of Bible study but of a different type of religious activity. Of course, the study of Scripture should lead to prayer, and some sort of prayer should be included in every meeting; but that does not mean that it is useful to intertwine prayer and Scripture into a single activity. When the Scripture is used in group prayer, what usually happens is that favourite passages are used again and again and that which is unfamiliar hardly ever enters; the eighth chapter of Romans is overworked and the thirteenth chapter of Zechariah is ignored. Such meetings can help a person to use Scripture and to love it, but in a very limited way. In fact, the participants' knowledge of the Bible is very seldom increased; what grows is their awareness of a passage already known. Prayer meetings will not so consistently conjure up the mental efforts necessary to learning, and learning is a vital part of catechesis.

The second possibility, a tantalising one, is the *creative activity* group. The group involved would certainly need to have a great lack of inhibitions with one another, so the group would either have to be a small collection of like-minded people or a small group who already knew each other well. The central idea is to get the members of the group to interact with the text itself by putting themselves into the roles of the characters in the text, paraphrasing passages, acting out a scene from the text in mime, or producing drawings inspired by some aspect of the text. All of this is mixed with guided discussion. If this is the type of structure which you envisage for your own group, you should investigate Walter Wink's *Transforming Bible Study* (published by Abingdon and SCM Press). He not only will give you a few ideas how such sessions should go, but a whole philosophy for taking such an approach in the first place.

After you have decided on the general approach and style of session your group will have, many of the other matters will fall into place naturally and other decisions will come more easily. If you are uncertain about the choice you have made, don't worry − it can always be changed. In such a case, you might want to ask the group themselves, but don't be too hasty about such an opinion poll. Make certain to give them a fair taste of the method which you think that you will be most comfortable with first; then if there are any suggestions they will not be coming out of a vacuum. However, the cardinal rule remains: the leader must never allow himself or herself to be landed with an approach with which he or she is basically uncomfortable. The group members will find it far easier to adapt to a structure than the group leader will.

3. What Type of Group?

4   What Do We Read?

Having decided to form your group, and having decided on the basic structure which you hope the meetings will take, you are not unlike a traveller with passport and ticket in your pocket ready for three weeks in some exotic land. What do you do once you get there? Are you going to hack your way through equatorial jungles, explore the by-ways off the beaten track, gape into the smouldering mouth of a volcano? Or are you going to remain in your four-star hotel, sipping the same drinks which you sip at home and refusing to sample any food which might not have come from your own kitchen? When some Bible groups form, they head straight for the passages and books which they already know and stay firmly implanted in them as if anything beyond them were a threat and a danger.

This tendency we shall term the "One Book Temptation". In Bible groups all over the world, the following scenario takes place:

> Leader: "Now that we have formed our little group to study the Bible, we have to decide what we are going to look at in the coming weeks. Do any of you have any suggestions?"
> Group Member (timidly): "Could we maybe study one of the gospels?"
> Rest of the Group (in chorus): "Wonderful! Fantastic! Great idea!"

No, I haven't sat in as a spy at the inaugural meeting of your group. It's just that, when faced with a choice, the vast majority of people (including Bible group leaders) will choose the familiar. In scriptural study that is a very dangerous tendency, for a number of reasons.

The first danger stems from the fact that most people beginning Scripture study have definite preconceptions of what Scripture is. They hold these preconceptions because of the parts of Scripture they already know, and if they confine themselves to those parts for group study they can complete their study of the Bible with the same misconceptions that they had to start with. If a person, for example, thinks that all of Scripture is composed of sacred stories which are undeviating

The dreaded one book temptation

in their historical accuracy, their misconception will never be challenged by the study of one gospel in isolation. If our potential biblical student is convinced that Scripture is full of "so-and-so begat so-and-so", then the worst fears will be confirmed upon reading the first chapter of Matthew's Gospel.

Then there is always the danger of never becoming aware of anything but the familiar, just more familiar of old friends. Scripture is a whole treasure-house of riches; it would be a shame to be content with a few nuggets lying close to the door when there are diamonds and rubies not too much farther inside. A little toying with the unfamiliar will shed new and exciting light even on the familiar passages.

The saddest possibility of the "One Book Temptation" is that none of the group will ever enter into the biblical way of thinking. Now everyone knows that the Scriptures were written long ago in languages different to our own. To some, this fact makes the Scriptures ancient curiosities, of very little relevance to modern circumstances. Other people more or less ignore this fact, and consequently the Bible becomes a very strange book, in some places not making sense at all and in others saying things which it never intended on saying. It is this latter group which bring out their pocket calculators and decide that the world will end in October of some year in the near future.

To enter into the biblical way of thinking completely is beyond our realistic goals; yet we can try to look at life the same way that the biblical authors did. To the extent to which we succeed, Scripture will become alive, the characters of its narratives will take on flesh and blood, and its wisdom will have piercing insights into our own lives. But that will never happen when you restrict your study to a book which you already half know off by heart.

Let's go back to our exotic holiday, and say that the purpose of your stay is to write an article on the people of Gumbigumbiland. So the first thing you do is to get away from your guide, wander into the non-tourist areas of the city, escape into the remote rural villages. Then, once seated at your typewriter, you can translate your experiences into terms which people who stray no further than the butcher's can

understand. But what happens if you spend the three weeks without leaving the comfort of the hotel's air-conditioning? "My extensive travels reveal that the native population of Gumbigumbiland have great difficulty in making a bed properly. The native costume of the men seems to be short white jackets which are constantly worn when bringing the esteemed foreign visitor the traditional dinner of roast beef and horseradish sauce." If you want to discover, you have to explore.

The one book approach does have its uses: it seems the one most suited to academic purposes. Courses in Scripture which form part of a larger course in theology have long included titles like "The Gospel of St Luke", "Paul's First Letter to the Corinthians", and so on. But these always form part of a series; these one book courses presume that the student will work through other courses on different books. For the general sort of Bible group which we are dealing with in this book, the "One Book Temptation" is best resisted.

There are two aspects of the "One Book Temptation" which might be useful all the same. One is that previous acquaintance can be capitalised on as long as it does not become a fence across which one can not pass. A good plan will always be a mixture of the familiar and the unfamiliar, and the familiar might well predominate; but the unfamiliar will be there as well, to expand the horizons and to add seasonings even to the familiar fare. The other cue we take from the "One Book Temptation" is that it can be rewarding to study a text in depth, but more on that later.

We leave the "One Book Temptation" to return to our eavesdropping on the inaugural meeting of an unnamed Bible group:

> Leader: "Yes, well, we might include one of the gospels in the material we study. But we don't want to restrict ourselves to parts of the Bible that we know already — even though there is quite a bit that we can learn about them. Actually, I had a suggestion on my own..."
> (Group members begin to look at each other nervously.)

Leader: ". . . which I hope won't seem too adventurous to you."

(Some members shift in their seats while others begin reaching for their coats.)

Leader: "I was hoping that we might spend some of our time looking at the Old Testament."

(Pandemonium breaks out as group members discover in their attempts to escape that the leader has locked and bolted the doors and windows.)

The Bible may be a bestseller, but it is one of those that never gets the first part read. Christians by and large have a definite anti-Old Testament bigotry, as if whatever is worthwile reading in Scripture is all to be found in the New Testament. No one would dispute that studying the New Testament is on the whole an easier business than studying its elder brother. It seems to be always talking about Jesus and the Christians, for one thing. For another, it seems more intelligible — less strange names, more familiar, more applicable to everyday living. What possible reason could any group have for spending time with the Old Testament when the New Testament is there, crying out to be read?

One reason for studying the Old Testament is precisely because we are interested in the New. When the apostles went out, preaching the Good News of Jesus, they were not carrying New Testaments under their arms. Their Bible was the Old Testament; it was in those pages (or scrolls, to be more precise) that they found the written Word of God. And whenever the New Testament refers to "the Scriptures" it is referring back to the Old Testament. The Old Testament shed the light in which the first century Christians saw the words and work of Jesus. The Old Testament also gives the New Testament some of its richest imagery and vocabulary; it is a grammar for the language that the New Testament speaks. The image of the Good Shepherd in John depends on the picture of God as shepherd of Israel in Ps 23 as well as the picture of the disappointing hireling shepherds, the political leaders of Israel, in the Book of Ezekiel. The richness and force of many new Testament passages will never even be seen, let alone appreciated, by the person who does not also read the Old Testament.

Then, too, there are striking pictures of what true religion means in the Old Testament which are presumed by the New Testament and not reproduced there. St Paul is very strong on faith and its value, but he roots his picture of faith in the stories of Abraham in the Book of Genesis. That primitive nomad might leave a lot to be desired by some Christian standards, but few Christians can match his utter faith; his powerful odyssey of trust still can help to guide our own pilgrimages. We need the psalms to teach us praise and a sense of wonder, perhaps even how to pray. If we tear the Old Testament from our Bibles, if not in reality at least for all practical purposes, how can we ever replace the outrage of the prophets at social injustice or their subtle lessons on hope? The treasures of Scripture are not confined to the pages of the New Testament.

One misgiving that some have about the Old Testament is that "it's not Christian". Certainly they have a point with some passages which are full of wrath and the cry for vengeance. Yet these can be read and appreciated without having to take away any of the violent attitudes as a lesson for one's own life. Every Easter Vigil we hear the story of the liberation of Israel from Egypt, yet very few are struck at all by the rather violent end of Pharoah's forces; what we take away from that reading is the mighty action of God on behalf of his people, that their hopes in him are not unfounded. As if we were eating peanuts, we rightly chew the meat and throw away the shell, nearly without thinking.

Then, too, we should remember the purpose of the Old Testament: it is meant to take people from a situation far from God and to lead them, step by step, to him — to prepare people for the full message of God made known in Jesus. Though I may not like to admit it, there is a lot which is non-Christian in me, a lot which needs something to prepare me to hear the word of Jesus in a particular corner of my own life. The Old Testament can speak to that part of me when the New Testament would fall on deaf ears. The love commandments of the New Testament are wonderful, but they can be empty platitudes if I still need to learn the lessons of social justice and human dignity from the Old Testament.

If people feel confused by what they hear in Scripture, it is usually a problem with the Old Testament. Either they are perplexed by a passage from the Old Testament itself or by something in the New Testament which depends on the Old Testament. Those who are puzzled by the vision of God's throne in the fourth chapter of Revelation are in fact being puzzled by the picture of God's throne in the opening chapter of Ezekiel. People who can make no sense of Stephen's speech in Acts 7:2-53 are confused by their own unfamiliarity with Old Testament history and its flow. The only way to disperse the confusion, or at least part of it, is to grasp the nettle and open a few pages of the Old Testament from time to time.

There still remains the problem of how best to use the Old Testament in the type of Bible group which we have in mind. If the programme of study is a longish one (lasting roughly the length of the academic year), then there should be some room in it to study the Old Testament for its own merits. Who could begrudge four sessions to the Book of Psalms or a half-dozen to the prophets? At the same time, the leader should not allow the Old Testament to predominate; most people do find it more of a strain and are more anxious to learn about the New Testament anyway.

Study of the Old Testament can also be tied in more closely with study of the New. Sessions on Old Testament passages can precede those on related New Testament passages. If a group plans to spend some time on chapters one to eight of Romans, the few sessions which they might spend on the stories of Abraham in Gen 12-25 will not go astray. The covenant recorded in Ex 19-24 would be a good introduction to the Sermon on the Mount, both as background and as contrast.

If the length of the course does not permit time to be given to the Old Testament on its own, there is one more way in which it can be brought to the attention of group members: there are few passages of any length in the New Testament which do not make reference to something in the Old Testament. Some of these cross references should be explored from time to time,

bringing out some of the allusions and overtones which the New Testament passage gains from its Old Testament resonances. Of course, if Old Testament study is restricted to this, the Old Testament will remain largely a closed book, but at least the group members will know that it is there and that it has some relevance to the New Testament.

After the whole issue of what to read is resolved, we still have to decide the rate at which we take it. Some groups deal with only a few verses at a time while others take sections of a few chapters every session. Which is it to be, fast or slow?

The fast approach will give the beginning group a wide overview of what is in the Bible and an appreciation of its variety. With a fast rate of reading, a patchwork quilt of passages can be built up in a relatively short time; the group can taste a sample of Old Testament Law, St Paul, the prophets and more within a few short weeks. It was this type of wide exposure which Vatican II had in mind when it called for the treasures of the Scriptures to be opened to the people in the Liturgy of the Word.

Yet the fast approach can have its disadvantages, too. If the group is studying something already somewhat familiar — say one of the gospels — might not the fast approach be a little too superficial? Perhaps a slower rate could bring out the depths which had gone unnoticed previously. The slower approach could also take advantage of the previous familiarity and build upon it. Besides, so much of scriptural scholarship is based on in-depth study of passages, the slower rate could be used to give the group a small sampling of the type of insights which scholarship gives us.

If the programme is long enough, there should be room for both rates of study to appear. First would come the quicker rate which would give a grounding in some of the different materials to be found in Scripture with excursions into both Testaments, then would come a slower study of something which is already half-familiar to the members of the group. If we are speaking about a programme for beginners, then we want to choose material which is representative of other material in the Bible, so that by studying it, other passages in the Scripture become more accessible to the group as well. There should also be some respect for the type of material which appears in the Liturgy of the Word; some members will have as one of their highest priorities the better understanding of what they hear on a Sunday morning.

The second part of this book sets out a sample programme for a beginners' Bible group lasting twenty-two sessions. It begins with a nine-session fast-approach over-view which touches on the Law, the Prophets, the Psalms and the New Testament Letters. After this comes a slower rate study of the Gospel of John which continues for thirteen sessions. Such a programme, with its mixture of fast and slow and Old and New, serves both to introduce the group to the unfamiliar and to get them to explore what may already be familiar in greater depth. We'll pay one last call to that inaugural meeting:

(The Leader is now cornered by an angry mob of twenty enraged group members. In one last desperate attempt to calm them and restore the rule of reason, he speaks.)
Leader: "You don't understand! I didn't plan on spending the whole time on the Old Testament, just a bit , just a tiny bit!"
Burly Group Member (through gritted teeth and in no mood for compromise): "Just how much time are you planning on spending on this Old Testament?"

Leader: "Seven sessions... no, six, SIX! Just half a dozen short sessions. You'd hardly even notice them!"
(It begins to work. An elderly member lowers the chair leg she had been brandishing. A member with training in first aid quits tightening the tourniquet he had applied to the Leader's neck.)
Suspicious Member: "And all of the other sessions we would work with the New Testament?"
Leader: "YES! YES!"
(The whole group begins to calm visibly, with the exception of the Leader.)
College Student Member (still coyly fingering the edge of her switchblade): "And we'd do a gospel?"
Leader (unsuccessfully trying to fight down the nervous tendency to shout): "DEFINITELY... Gospel of John... lovely gospel, you'll all love John, I know... THIRTEEN SESSIONS, more than double what we would spend on... er, the, uh, more ancient parts of the Bible... a gospel, definitely... wouldn't be Bible study without a gospel!"
Burly Group Member (taking charge): "Well, that sounds fair to me. How does it sound to the rest of you?"
(Murmured agreement from most of the other nineteen)
"Okay, Mrs Winston, you can untie him. It's time to break for that cup of tea, anyway."

5 The Group and its Members

Between the time when it is first announced that there will be a Bible study group starting and the actual first coming together of the group, many potential group leaders complain of a vivid, recurring nightmare:

> It is the night of the first meeting, and I go to the venue which we had announced. I set out fifteen chairs in a semi-circle, look at them and decide that it isn't enough. I set out a second semi-circle of eighteen chairs behind the first row and wait. The appointed time comes, but no one has arrived.
>
> "It's a bad night to come out into", I say to myself, even though it is warm and the moon shines in a cloudless sky. Ten minutes later I have just about decided to go back home when the door opens slowly, and a woman in her early thirties looks in.
>
> "Is this where the picture study class meets?" she inquires.
>
> "Scripture study" I answer. "It's a group for studying the Bible."
>
> "Oh, I though it was looking at pictures", she says not trying to hide her disappointment, and leaves.
>
> That is the point where I always wake up.

So far we have succeeded in speaking of the Bible study group without too much reference to the people who will make it up. Naturally, who becomes a member of the group and who doesn't is a matter of that person's decision, not of yours. At the same time, it might be useful to keep a few ideals and pointers in mind, even if it is not always possible to implement all of them.

If the effort is really one to provide an opportunity for adults to discover more about their faith, then membership of the group should be open to all. If the group is parish based, then publicity for it should be a parish effort; an announcement or two from the altar on Sunday, notice in the parish newsletter, a poster in the church porch can all get across the message that this Bible group is open to all comers, not just to a spiritual or intellectual elite.

But to dissipate that recurring nightmare, something more

As you plan more and more for the group people who might be interested come to mind.

might be done. As you plan more and more for the group, people who might be interested will come to mind. There is no harm in approaching a number of these to issue a personal invitation. Some won't be as interested as you would have thought; others will jump at the opportunity. In this way you will form a small core group on whose initial participation you can rely.

Since you have control over the matter of precisely whom you invite in this way, we could here consider what sort of a mixture a good group should have. I referred briefly in chapter three to groups which are drawn from a well defined base with

29

a common interest; there would be groups for youth or the retired and groups which grow out of another activity, for instance, groups of those involved in the charismatic movement or from a sodality. Groups of people sharing a common background in this way can have their advantages: they can be more supportive of one another and so be less inhibited; it is far easier to decide on approach with such a group, and perhaps even the material from Scripture to be studied will suggest itself even more clearly. Our basic concern, however, is here with the general group, not the special interest one.

In fact, a good mixture can add considerably to the richness of the group experience. Young and old, male and female are obvious contrasts to aim for. But the mix should be wider than that: professional people and working class, pragmatic and theoretical, those with a faith geared towards traditional devotion, those with a faith geared more towards social reform – they all have something exciting to show each other in the Word of God, and a few surprises to spring on the group leader, too. The membership of the group should reflect the mixture of the local community from which it is formed.

When you approach your "invitees", keep this mixture in mind so that your invitations are not all issued to like-minded people from identical backgrounds. Another way in which to encourage the mixture is to make certain that the general invitation is repeated in a variety of special interest groups already active in the parish. An invitation given by the leader at, say, the rehearsal of the parish folk group is nearly as good as a personal invitation given to each member, although the scope to decline the invitation is much wider. Remember as you work to ensure your group membership has a cross-section of the community that the potential of the group increases as the mixture becomes more varied.

Perhaps size is a factor over which you as group leader have even less control, but one which is very relevant to the type of group which you will have. The *guided discussion* group is limited to a maximum of about ten members; any more than that and some will become spectators and even the number of

members will become a threat to stifle some contributions. If the numbers slip beneath half a dozen then the sessions can degenerate from discussion into conversation; discussions are hard enough to keep on the track, but conversations will only touch the point once *every* quarter of an hour. You can nearly hear the hobby-horses neighing.

Those sessions which have a greater emphasis on input (the *teach-in* and *talk and discussion* types) can cater for a larger number of members and can work with anything up to thirty-five or forty members. Even in this situation, though, as the numbers increase, so do the inhibitions and the formality. Ideally the group should be small enough for the members to get to know one another, and that puts the number to aim for at about twenty.

Of course, the group that actually turns up may be smaller than the twenty which I just mentioned. Don't be deceived into thinking that the usefulness of a Bible study group is determined by the number of people who attend the meetings. There is always the ripple effect: the stone that is dropped into the pond not only creates an initial splash but also concentric ripples which eventually spread out to the water's edge. The session is the initial splash which the Word of God makes, those with whom the group members live, work, even meet, get the ripples. Who can measure the effect it has on the family home when mother starts reading the Bible? Even when the television is not broken? Then, too, we can get so wound up in the numbers game that we forget the benefit which an activity can be to those who are present. Instead of being thankful that there are a number of people interested in furthering their Christian education and that this need is being catered for in a small way, we bemoan the multitude who aren't there. Once I was in a parish where a Bible group was formed at the same time that a survey was carried out in the parish on many subjects. According to the result of that survey, some two to three hundred people were definitely interested in becoming members of a parish Bible study group; we started with a dozen members. As one sage phrased it, "Man counts heads, God counts hearts".

"Moses, the time has come. I want all the Hebrews to get ready to leave Egypt for good and to go to the Promised Land. It's up to you to get them organised so that everything is ready when Pharoah gives the word. He won't be long in changing his mind, so I want all people on the move at once."

"Lord, hold on a minute. I've been giving this whole exodus thing a bit of thought and... Well, we're going out to that Promised Land, right?"

"Right."

"Which isn't exactly down the road. And we're going to be a new nation, right?"

"Right."

"Lord, I was thinking, there's no need to bring everybody. We'll pick out those with useful skills, the hunters, the tentmakers, the herders. We'll get rid of some of the dead weight so that the group can move quickly, and..."

"Moses, don't worry about how fast you go. Just get the people ready to move out."

"Lord, this is our chance to weed out the undesirables. The criminal element has no place in this new nation under your Law."

"Good. First we get rid of all those who were up for the manslaughter of Egyptians who beat Hebrew workers."

"Let's not get personal, Lord."

"No, Moses, we take them all, the able-bodied and the feeble, the useful and the troublesome. When I say 'My People', I mean *all* my people."

"Could we at least leave Shiphrah, the midwife, behind? Lord, that woman is always complaining about something. Only the other day she was saying that dandruff would have made a much better plague than frogs. I said to her..."

Every group has its problem members, and every group leader is wise to be prepared for them, at least to recognise that they exist.

The one type of problem member which is sure to be represented is the member who always finds something better to discuss than the matter in hand. Actually, this type has two distinct species: one species flitters lightly from subject to subject, dipping here, sipping there, sometimes touching as many as five completely different topics in one intervention; the second is zealous in searching for wisps of the discussion which will serve as fodder for the hobby-horse. The treatment is the same for both: surgery with (or, if absolutely necessary, without) anaesthetic. Practise saying some of these phrases in front of a mirror forty or fifty times:

> "I think that we've strayed slightly from the point here; could we just get back to..."
> "That question isn't precisely on what we've been talking about, so I'll just try to answer it very quickly, and then we can get back to the prophet Isaiah."
> "What you have been saying about saving the whale is all very interesting, but I don't think that it is quite the message of the story of Noah, Mrs Flood."
> "Jamie, could I just stop you there and ask the group: does anyone see in this passage from Amos a *different* solution to our present social difficulties from Jamie's suggestion of violent revolution?"

While it might seem kinder to let the distractionist traipse merrily down the country lanes, remember that the rest of the group might be in agony — especially if the distractionist performs these sleight-of-mouth tricks at nearly every session. Sometimes the leader can use the boredom of the group when other attempts have failed, by throwing the topic open to other contributions; if none are forthcoming, the discussion can move on.

In fact, all but the most hardened distractionists will respond to a bit of discipline. If firm but gentle measures are taken early on, the problem will lessen as the group matures.

Other people will come to the sessions with problems of faith, and this is a very healthy thing both for the group and for the person himself. There could be no better source of light to throw on problems of faith than the Word of God. At different times, many members of the group will bring out their own problems of faith and understanding, and the group — especially the group leader — will try to assist as best they can. The situation becomes unhealthy, though, when one group member has a faith problem to which he is constantly trying to convert the rest of the group. Let's imagine that Carl gets it into his head that God the Father has a physical body; the reading material at every session becomes added proof that his suspicion is well-founded: "There, it says 'with mighty hand and out-stretched arm.' How can you have a hand and arm without a physical body?" If Carl's notions are left undented by explanations of metaphor and suchlike, if the matter raises its hairy head at every session, then it might be well to have a more private talk with Carl. The absence of an audience might help him to see the point; if not, then the leader might think it wise to tell Carl that his contributions on this point don't seem to be too useful to the other members of the group, and that it might be an idea to drop the subject for a few sessions. Even though God the Father's physical body goes unmentioned for a few weeks, the leader should not forget about the problem but try to help Carl more indirectly, perhaps by lingering a bit on some text concerning God's transcendence. Never enlarge the size of a stumbling block by making an issue of it, especially by making it an issue for public debate.

There is also the possibility that the Scripture study group will attract someone with severe personality problems. If the leader knows the person or the person's problems from some other contact, then the leader will be much more distracted by the presence of the problem member than the rest of the group; many members of the group may not be aware of any abnormalities at all. The group, like the Church itself, ought to be wide enough to include such a person, problems and all. The best strategy attempts to integrate the person as fully as possible into the group, often more of a possibility than the leader might imagine. Eccentric contributions are treated in much the same way as distractions of other types; if the leader is consistent in discouraging all straying from the matter at hand, no undue offence will be taken. If the problem member feels too constrained by this, he will leave without doing any real damage to the group; if he finds the group meeting helpful, he will stay, perhaps even gaining healing and support from the group itself. In any case, his presence should not be a source of worry to the group leader.

Most group members will not be problem members, however. In fact, the real definition of a problem member is one who causes more difficulties for the rest of the group than the leader himself does! The majority of the members will enrich and enhance the group. Each member's contributions will be supplemented and complemented by the contributions which follow, each person's horizons will be widened by the glimpses which he or she receives of someone else's vision. No member will ever go out of a session the poorer; most will leave a little richer in the treasures of the Word of God than when they entered. We could even include the group leader in that.

6 Aims and Practical Considerations

This final chapter of part one covers some of the practical odds and ends which we have avoided so far, questions such as time and length, the social side of the group, the place of prayer and so forth. But before we dive into these, we should have one final focusing on what a Bible group is all about.

It need hardly be said that one of the primary aims of a Bible study group is *educational*; the group is set up to give people an opportunity to learn about Scripture, and people come because they want to learn. This aim is served by the input which is given at the meeting, usually by the group leader.

If the sole aim of the group were educational, the whole affair would remain an intellectual exercise. But such is not the case, for closely related to the educational aim is a *formational* one: most of the members will have at least an indirect desire, not only to become better informed Christians by participating in the study group, but better Christians all round. For this reason the successful group is not one which only shows its members what such-and-such a passage meant when it was written, but one which also goes on to show what it means today. If the leader who is giving the input also tries to make this application for the group members, he resigns his role as leader of Scripture study and dons the robes of a homilist; it is up to the members themselves to make the applications and to share the insights which the Word of God gives them into living. The formational aim takes in the total experience of the group meetings, but is especially served by the interacting and sharing of the group members. The praying which a group might do together also is part of this formational aspect.

There is a more subtle and indirect aim, one which sometimes only emerges once the group is active, the *social* aim. It is only to be expected that people who come together out of a common interest (the Bible) should develop a sense of fellowship and unity over a certain period of time. As members begin to know one another and relax in each other's company as they begin to appreciate each other's insights and recognise each other's limitations, the discussions will take fire and Scripture will become more and more alive. Unfortunately, this process takes time; my own experience would lead me to think

that a group's social heart only begins to beat after the first year. But once it does take off, then the social aspect itself helps to serve both the educational and the formational aims of the group.

Our practical questions should be seen in light of these three aims. One or other option may be more appealing to the group leader, but the overriding concern should always be how best the educational, formational and social aspects of the meetings will emerge.

The first questions to arise are those of *time*, especially the length of the individual meeting, the frequency of the meetings, and the length of the course. As far as the length of an individual meeting goes, there is one unchanging maxim for me: an hour and a half. Anything more than that exceeds most people's attention span, anything less hardly seems worth coming out for on a wet winter's evening. It is no harm to be rigid in stopping at the appointed time, no matter how interesting the discussion or brilliant the monologue; there is a certain security in knowing as you enter the room at eight that you will be reaching for your coat at half-past-nine.

The best option for frequency of meetings seems to be once a week. The weekly meeting soon establishes itself in the routine of the members and best gives a sense of continuity to the work being done. Yet the weekly meeting is not the only option; the fortnightly meeting, for instance, lacks the regularity of the weekly session, but is not as demanding on the leader's time and energies. Meetings once a month are too distant from each other for the threads of the last session not to be lost. The only circumstance under which a monthly meeting should even be contemplated is where the Scripture session is fitting in with the routine of an already existing group; for instance, an informal prayer group might want to devote its meeting on the first Tuesday of every month to studying the Bible while the other meetings proceed as normal.

Then there is the major decision of how long the course of sessions should run. It is possible to have a short course of between four and six sessions, ideally suited for a special occasion, such as a series of Lenten lectures. Naturally, one should not expect too much to emerge on the social side during a short series; but it will get people started and will attract many who would not be prepared to make a longer commitment. A slightly larger commitment would be required for a course of two to three months, which would also give more of a chance to the social aspect of the group. If you have opted to ignore the impassioned pleadings of chapter four and decided to restrict the group to the study of one book, the course of two to three months is tailor-made to fit your needs.

A course which lasts roughly the length of an academic year best allows the group to achieve its fullest potential. Over the span of twenty to thirty working meetings, a number of topics can be covered and the group can be exposed to more than one or two books. Group members will develop working relationships with one another, learning to appreciate each other's vision and to accept each other's limitations. In the parish situation, a full year's running will establish the group as a feature of the locality, something to which people might feel drawn long after the opening sessions. The whole effort has broken through a definite barrier once the members start to think of Tuesday as "Bible night".

The sessions in the second part of the book sketch out a plan for the full year's course, twenty-two sessions in all. But they can also be divided in different ways. If you have decided on a short introductory course of six sessions, you could use the notes for Sessions I, IV, V, VI, VII and VIII to form an introductory look at the Old Testament. Or if the two to three month course fits your needs, Sessions X to XXII could be used as a unit on the Gospel of John, studied at a leisurely pace. If the whole course of twenty-two sessions is covered, it should give the beginner a fair experience of what Scripture is about and what it has to offer.

Another matter on the educational side of things which is best to consider before you exercise your leadership is the question of *audio-visual aids*. Don't let the term put you off. We might only be talking about a blackboard and a piece of chalk. Actually, the one aid which *every* member should have in the hand at *every* session is the Bible itself. An essential part of the experience of Bible study is getting the fingers working in tracking down a passage, in finding that Genesis is in the front and the Letters of John towards the back, to break that mysterious code of chapter and verse. Even the fact that different members are using different translations can come in useful when the leader wants to show that there is more than one way of translating a certain verse. Never underestimate the value of the teaching aid which is already in every member's possession.

But let's go back to the old stand-by of a blackboard and piece of chalk, what do you use them for, presuming that you have them? Certainly not to put all of your information on; all of your vast knowledge spilled out onto three yards of slate in cramped writing might seem too daunting to the poor unsuspecting member. No, we are talking about communication, not drilling information into people; whatever goes onto that board should serve as a focus around which they can mentally organise what is being said as well as their own reflections. So central words and ideas are the main things to write down. Other items also cry out to be written down, not because of their centrality but because of their unfamiliarity. If you do not want a term like synoptic to be forever remembered as "sin optic", it is safest to write it down. This applies especially to dates; there isn't much difference between 587 BC and 722 BC when the numbers are simply rattled off. Unless they can be seen, they might mentally be translated into "a very long time ago". If it is important enough to give the group a Greek or Hebrew word, it is important enough for them to see it in transliteration.

Apart from isolated words and numbers, there are other items which can be usefully written on the board. Lists of references, patterns of thought which emerge from the text, simple diagrams to show what is more important and what is less important, even a short list of central events with their dates are all candidates for a blackboard's space. Some of the charts included with the session notes in Part Two will give you a few ideas. If some of the group members are trying to keep notes of the session, then anything which is written up for them to see will be of immeasurable help.

If you are really one of the adventurous leaders, you might consider the use of an overhead projector. In most venues, this miracle of the technological age doesn't even need a screen: the image can simply be cast onto a plain wall of a lightish hue, or if there is a rather stout member wearing a plain shirt... The great advantage is that the material written on the transparencies is prepared beforehand, so there is no need to stop every so often to write things on the board; and the transparencies are kept, so that if the leader wishes to remind the group of something done in a previous session, then the transparency from that session can easily be produced. For a price, prepared transparencies can be purchased, although these tend to be expensive. An amazing machine, the overhead projector.

It should be possible to get the odd sheet of paper reproduced for the members of the group. To have notes prepared in this way for every session is probably not worth the considerable time and expense which goes into it; the sheets tend to get more and more ignored as their quantity increases. If these duplicated sheets are restricted to sheets which the group member will refer to again and again, especially outside of the actual meeting, they will be far more valuable. Perhaps a page could be prepared listing the reading material and the discussion questions for the next few sessions, or a sheet might give a chart with all of those confusing periods and personages of Old Testament history simplified into a time-line. But don't glut the market; we don't want to crack the binding of anyone's Bible with the generosity of our "handouts".

The odd film-strip, slides from a trip to the Holy Land, a map or two, and a dozen and one other possibilities might suggest themselves from time to time. Don't be afraid to use whatever is available to you; but you should never feel that you are not ready for a session if you are armed with no more than that piece of chalk. It will remain your trusty friend even when the slide projector gets jammed, there is no spirit in the spirit duplicator, and the bulb in the overhead projector dims inexplicably to five watts.

Some groups look to pre-recorded tapes to give the informational input to the session. If the group is quite small and there is no one available to address the group directly, then this approach can be quite successful. If, however, one of the group has some background, it would be far more desirable for that member to prepare a short input by a private listening to the tape, and then presenting the live input to the group in place of the pre-recorded cassette. Playing a tape to a sizeable group week after week just isn't on; but isolated tapes could be used from time to time to provide variety. Recorded music can play a part in the ordinary session, either music which uses a passage from the Bible as its inspiration (as in the musical *Godspel*) or a popular song which somehow reflects what a passage in Scripture is saying. Again, there is hardly reason for the tape-recorder to appear at every session, unless the group leader has an unbelievable collection of recorded material and a special charism for using it.

Every meeting of the Bible group, on the other hand, should find room for some sort of prayer. Exactly what type will depend on the group and the preferences of the members, but there are a number of possibilities to keep in mind.

The easiest way out is a short prayer at the start of the meeting, either a commonly known prayer recited together or a short collect (or similar) chosen from the many books of prayer available. The brief prayer might also be a spontaneous or prepared prayer based on the reading material for the session. The great drawback with this type of brief introductory prayer is that it hardly qualifies as prayer together. And prayer

The overhead projector doesn't always need a screen.

35

together is really what we want if we have the formational aim in mind.

The Liturgy of the Hours provides a form of prayer which is meant to be said together. While Evening Prayer would be the theoretical ideal, it is probably too adventurous for the majority of Bible groups, both in length and in complexity. Much more attractive to the person unfamiliar with the Office is Night Prayer. One of the two Sunday Night Prayers could be used as a base, perhaps taking the reading from the material which the group has been studying that night and introducing intercessions before the collect. If Night Prayer is celebrated in this way, it should take about ten minutes of the session.

Of course, there is nothing to prevent different models emerging. If spontaneous prayer open to the whole group is introduced, it should normally take place at the end of the meeting. The meeting itself will help to formulate this prayer, and the experience might teach some of the members how to bring their Scripture reading directly into their prayer life.

Or you might do what our local group is doing at present. Every meeting a person volunteers to prepare a reading for the following meeting (the last person to hide behind his or her chair is deemed volunteered); the reading comes from the Liturgy of the Word for the Sunday following. At the end of the session, we begin our prayer with half a minute's silence followed by a verse or two of a hymn. Then the reader says a word or two about the reading and reads it. Another half minute's silence concludes with the group reciting a psalm together, and then spontaneous prayers from members of the group, usually in the form of the Prayer of the Faithful at the Eucharist. When contributions to these have finished, there is a short prayer based on the reading chosen for the prayer session, and the meeting ends. It has the added benefit of preparing us for one of the readings on the Sunday to come.

Yes, I mentioned a hymn. No, we are not really a choir masquerading as a Scripture class. There is a very strong tradition of song in the biblical ideas of prayer, and there is no reason that it shouldn't find expression in a Bible group; if you don't believe the whole Book of Psalms, then look up Jms 5:13 or Eph 5:19 or even Mk 14:26. It helps to have a few words available, so that you don't find yourself singing "Holy God, We Praise Thy Name" every week.

There is one prayer event which should be the highlight of the course: the end of the year group Mass. If well prepared to bring together the efforts the group has been making for week after week, if it is celebrated with song and silence and place for spontaneous prayer and plenty of time, then it will be not only a crowning of the whole course but also an enriching of each member's love of the Eucharist. It also makes a wonderful climax on which to end the year's work.

We might now turn our attention to the *social side* of the Scripture group. The weekly meeting should be something to which the members look forward; we could go so far as to say that it should have some entertainment value. Not only should the members learn to enjoy each other's company, even while in pursuit of such a noble venture as Bible study, but the leader should not be above throwing in the odd pun or odd joke when it helps to make the point. Laughter is a sign of relaxation, and the material will penetrate further if the atmosphere is relaxed. It is up to the leader to create such an atmosphere and it is so easily done; unless, of course, you are the type who hasn't laughed in seventeen years. In that case, yoga might be more suitable to you than leading others in the discovery of the joys of Scripture. The sessions in Part Two purposely open with the Book of Jonah to remind people that even Scripture has its humorous moments.

Look for excuses to break the usual pattern of your meetings from time to time. If you can find a guest speaker (who can be even less of a biblical expert than you are), maybe to show a set of slides on the Holy Land, then the group can work together to provide a few cakes and buns to honour the invited guest. That gets people co-operating before you start, and you might discover that the person in the corner who seems too shy ever to speak comes into her own in organising a "spread". It also is bound to relax members with each other even more: it's hard to remain stiff and formal with someone you're dripping powdered sugar over.

A cup of tea or something stronger (coffee) might form part of every meeting. Of course, it entails a certain amount of inconvenience, but most people need the break. And break it should be, an opportunity to put aside whatever formality is in the meeting and to talk with the people around. Don't try to continue "business as usual" during the tea, talking over the clatter of cups and saucers and weaving around to be seen past the person going around with the milk and sugar. Let the cup of tea be a "buzz session", a time when people can talk over the evening's material in a very unstructured way. Make certain that the break doesn't go on for too long; if it can be confined to ten minutes, that's long enough.

There are other things which the group can do together during the usual time for meeting. A Passover meal is an eye-opener to many, and there are books telling you how to do it (the Passover *Haggadah*) freely available. Or perhaps a service of readings and lights before Christmas could be composed. Outside of the meeting, the group might want to spend a day's retreat together, if a suitable venue and retreat master can be found. If there are a few groups near to each other, they might meet once in a while. In the Dublin area for the past few years there has been such a day of study and prayer organised which is now eagerly looked forward to by many groups. And all of this contributes not just to the social aspect, but to the educational and formational aims of the group as well.

Above all, keep those three aims in mind for your group and you'll hardly go wrong. If you find that you have given the group nothing new in their approach to Scripture, then you have forgotten the educational aim. If people are not getting to know the Lord and their own Christianity better, you have neglected the formational aim. If people are not getting to know each other within the group, the social aim has been cast aside.

And you'll find yourself benefiting from those aims, too. You yourself will be learning all the time; you yourself will find your own Christianity deepening. You might even discover yourself looking forward to the meetings if you aren't careful.

A Note on Translations

A question sure to arise in any Bible study group is "What is the best translation?" Translations differ so widely, and have been produced in such abundance in more recent times, that the question will not permit a single answer. We will take inventory of some of the translations which are more likely to appear in your group, and point out some of their strengths and weaknesses.

Most of the Bible is written in the contemporary language of the people who first listened to it. That alone is an argument against using the sixteenth and seventeenth century translations of Scripture. The language has moved on considerably since they were produced; so has the science of translation. They still remain the choice of some readers of Scripture, largely for sentimental reasons. As the Word of God becomes more alive for them, these readers often change to a more contemporary rendering.

The *Revised Standard Version* (often referred to as the *RSV*) is a revision of the most famous of these older translations, the *Authorised Version* (or *King James Version*). Although it is basically a modern translation, it retains some of the vocabulary and even archaisms of its predecessor, and so can be difficult for the beginner to read. It tries to be a very literal translation, and for that reason it is beloved of many biblical scholars. A Catholic edition of the *RSV* has been available for many years, yet explanatory notes and cross references are scarce in the Catholic edition. Because of its attempt to be as literal as possible, it is often used as a base translation for commentaries.

The *Jerusalem Bible* is a more modern translation which is much freer than the *RSV*, but generally a faithful translation; although in some books (such as the First Letter to the Corinthians) it can be quite disappointing. It is a translation from the original languages produced by Catholic scholars, but in ambiguous passages (as well as for its introductions and notes) it follows *la Bible de Jerusalem*, a famous French version produced by the Jerusalem *École Biblique*. Among the consultors for the English language style was the famous Tolkien. There are useful introductions and notes in all editions, but the *Standard Edition* is outstanding for its cross references, solid introductions and extensive explanatory notes; it has been compared to a text and small commentary in one volume.

The *New International Version* is also truly a modern version, but one which often follows the interpretation of the *Authorised Version*, even in places where that interpretation is quite dubious. It has no study aids, no notes, no cross references, and because it was produced by an interdenominational team of conservative Protestant translators, there is no edition available with the deuterocanonical books (those books of Scripture which Catholics accept but which most Protestants do not).

The *New American Bible* tries to strike a balance between a strict translation and the flow of modern English. It has notes which many beginners find quite useful and a number of cross references to other biblical passages. Although not without its faults, this modern Catholic translation seems a very suitable working Bible for those who want a text to read and study.

The *New English Bible* attempts a polished, timeless English. It doesn't always work. The *New English Bible* retains archaic speech in prayer and sometimes changes the Old Testament text in a way best described as mauling. Most editions are published without any study aids, although the deuterocanonical books are available in the editions published "with the Apocrypha".

The *Good News Bible* (also called *Today's English Version*) is also available in an edition "with the Apocrypha". It calls itself a "dynamic translation", which means that it is freer in interpreting the meaning of a text as it translates. Its very modern English makes for fast, easy reading, but its freedom with the text means that caution must be exercised when pulling a short passage from it. It has a few study aids, among the best being the simple line drawings which accompany the text in most editions. If you look for the poetry of the Bible in its pages, though, you might be disappointed.

The so-called *Living Bible* (also published as *The Way*) is not a Bible at all, but a paraphrase of the *Authorised Version*. Ideas can enter into it which are not part of the Scriptures. For the purposes of Scripture study, it should never be touched.

This brief review might end with a taste of the translations mentioned. It won't give you much of an idea of what sort of cross references or footnotes go with the text, or how hard the type is to read. The only way to discover if a particular Bible suits you is to use it for a considerable period of time. Even then, never be afraid to change; there is no such thing as the perfect translation.

Our survey will take two passages in each translation, a familiar gospel passage (Jn 17:21-23) and a less familiar passage from Paul (I Thess 2:17-20). We'll begin with the *Authorised Version* as an example of an older translation:

> That they all may be one; as thou, Father, *art* in me, and I in thee, that they also may be one in us: that the world may believe that thou hast sent me. And the glory which thou gavest me I have given them; that they may be one, even as we are one: I in them and thou in me, that they may be made perfect in one; and that the world may know that thou hast sent me, and hast loved them, as thou hast loved me.

> But we, brethren, being taken from you for a short time in presence, not in heart, endeavoured the more abundantly to see your face with great desire. Wherefore we would have come unto you, even I Paul, once and again; but Satan hindered us. For what *is* our hope, or joy, or crown of rejoicing? *Are* not *even* ye in the presence of our Lord Jesus Christ at his coming? For ye are our glory and joy.

Secondly, the *Revised Standard Version:*

> That they may all be one; even as thou, Father, art in me, and I in thee, that they also may be in us, so that the world may believe that thou hast sent me. The glory which thou hast given me I have given to them, that they may be one even as we are one, I in them and thou in me, that they may become perfectly one, so that the world may know that thou hast sent me and hast loved them even as thou hast loved me.

> But since we were bereft of you, brethren, for a short time, in person not in heart, we endeavoured the more eagerly and with great desire to see you face to face; because we wanted to come to you — I, Paul, again and again — but Satan hindered us. For what is our hope or joy or crown of boasting before our Lord Jesus at his coming? Is it not you? For you are our glory and joy.

The *Jerusalem Bible* is next; it arranges the gospel passage in sense-lines:

> May they all be one.
> Father, may they be one in us,
> as you are in me and I am in you,
> so that the world may believe it was you who sent me.
> I have given them the glory you gave to me,
> that they may be one as we are one.
> With me in them and you in me,
> may they be so completely one
> that the world will realise that it was you who sent me
> and that I have loved them as much as you loved me.

> A short time after we had been separated from you — in body but never in thought, brothers — we had an especially strong desire and longing to see you face to face again, and we tried hard to come and visit you; I, Paul, tried more than once, but Satan prevented us. What do you think is our pride and our joy? You are; and you will be *the* crown of which we shall be *proudest* in the presence of our Lord Jesus when he comes; you are our pride and our joy.

Now the *New International Version:*

> That all of them may be one, Father, just as you are in me and I am in you. May they also be in us so that the world may believe that you have sent me. I have given them the glory that you gave me, that they may be one as we are one: I in them and you in me. May they be brought to complete unity to let the world know that you sent me and have loved them even as you have loved me.

39

But, brothers, when we were torn away from you for a short time (in person, not in thought), out of our intense longing we made every effort to see you. For we wanted to come to you — certainly I, Paul, did, again and again — but Satan stopped us. For what is our hope, our joy, or the crown in which we will glory in the presence of our Lord Jesus Christ when he comes? Is it not you? Indeed, you are our glory and joy.

The *New American Bible* also opts for sense-lines for the Johannine passage:

That all may be one
as you, Father, are in me, and I in you;
I pray that they may be (one) in us,
that the world may believe that you sent me.
I have given them the glory you gave me
that they may be one, as we are one —
I living in them, you living in me —
that their unity may be complete.
So shall the world know that you sent me,
and that you loved them as you loved me.

Brothers, when we were orphaned by separation from you for a time — in sight, not in mind — we were seized with the greatest longing to see you. So we tried to come to you — I, Paul, tried more than once — but Satan blocked the way. Who, after all, if not you, will be our hope or joy, or the crown we exult in, before our Lord Jesus Christ at his coming? You are our boast and our delight.

Next, the sample from the *New English Bible:*

May they all be one: as thou, Father, art in me, and I in thee, so also may they be in us, that the world may believe

that thou didst send me. The glory which thou gavest me I have given to them, that they may be one, as we are one; I in them and thou in me, may they be perfectly one. Then the world will learn that thou didst send me, that thou didst love them as thou didst me.

My friends, when for a short spell you were lost to us — lost to sight, not to our hearts — we were exceedingly anxious to see you again. So we did propose to come to Thessalonica — I, Paul, more than once — but Satan thwarted us. For after all, what hope or joy or crown of pride is there for us, what indeed but you, when we stand before our Lord Jesus at his coming? It is you who are indeed our glory and our joy.

Finally, the *Good News Bible:*

I pray that they may all be one, Father! May they be in us, just as you are in me and I am in you. May they be one, so that the world will believe that you sent me. I gave them the same glory you gave me, so that they may be one, just as you and I are one: I in them and you in me, so that they may be completely one, in order that the world may know that you sent me and that you love them as you love me.

As for us, brothers, when we were separated from you for a little while — not in our thoughts, of course, but only in body — how we missed you and how hard we tried to see you again! We wanted to return to you. I myself tried to go back more than once, but Satan would not let us. After all, it is you — you, no less than others! — who are our hope, our joy, and our reason for boasting of our victory in the presence of our Lord Jesus when he comes. Indeed, you are our pride and our joy!

Part Two

An Itinerary for Bible Study

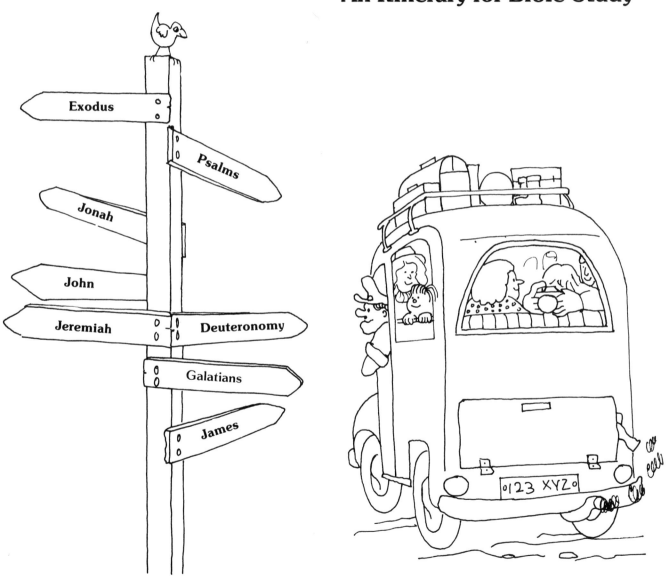

Introducing Part Two

This second section is designed to give the group leader a plan for studying the Bible over twenty-two weekly sessions, the first few sessions making a general tour of major parts of Scriptures and the remaining sessions involving a more detailed study of the Gospel of John.

Each session begins with an essay to give the group leader some bearings on the material for the session. Often the essay considers an aspect of Scripture wider than the scope of the biblical material for the session, but relevant to it; this is especially true of the first ten sessions.

After the essay follows a set of notes intended for use during the session itself. These always reflect the content of the essay as well as the reading material from Scripture; a few comments on verses of the scriptural material form part of these notes, as well as possible questions for group discussion. At the end of every session the reading material and discussion questions for the next session are noted so that the group leader can give them to group members as preparation work for the next meeting.

Each leader will have his or her own approach to using this part of the book. The essay is designed for reading before any detailed examination of the Scripture passage. After reading the essay the scriptural text itself should be studied, keeping in mind some of the points from the essay. Then the session notes could be examined and the comments on the text read with the passage close to hand. If the book is to be brought to the meeting, those session notes which seem especially important should be marked with a pen or pencil.

As mentioned in chapter six, it is possible to produce courses of different lengths by using these sessions in different ways:

Sessions I, IV, V, VI, VII and VIII could form a short series of six meetings which would give a basic course on the Old Testament.

Sessions X to XII give material for a longer series on the Gospel of John.

All twenty-two sessions provide the basis for a first year's group study of the Bible.

Introducing the Bible
The Book of Jonah

The first meeting of the group is bound to be clumsy; even the session notes are a bit clumsy, trying to cover two quite different areas. On the first night the leader is apprehensive. The group members will have different feelings, ranging from expectant enthusiasm all the way down to regret that they've come at all.

Obviously, the first thing to centre on is the one thing which gives this embryonic group its unity: the Bible, its nature and purpose. In a sense, though, that is the work of the entire series of Bible group sessions. So in giving an introduction to this you are presenting an introduction to the whole year's work.

Perhaps the initial point to get across is that everyone in the group has some familiarity with the Bible already: they have been listening to parts of it for years, know some short verses off by heart, are familiar with many of its characters — and this means that everyone in the group has something to contribute. Yet there is much in the Scriptures to be discovered by everyone in the group (including the leader!), which is the whole purpose of the group. This journey of discovery is not a study of history, nor a quest for a font of ancient wisdom, but a study of Scripture as the Word of God.

Calling the Scripture the *Word* of God doesn't mean that it is a series of quotations from him. *Word* here means *revelation*, God telling us about himself and about us, and about the two together. The Scriptures are part of a conversation between God and man, not pontificating statements issued by a press officer. God's Word is meant to be a way for us to get to know God, not just about God. That's why the Bible is not just a book to be read like a novel, but a book to be pondered and argued with, a book to haunt and enchant us, until it enters into our very way of thinking.

But then again, the Bible isn't a book at all — it's a whole collection of books. There's poetry and philosophy in it, historical material and bits that are nearer to fiction. It's not even all written in one language, but three (Hebrew, Aramaic and Greek), and in places as far removed as Jerusalem, Rome, and Babylon. It took over thirteen hundred years for the material to take the form it has now, which means that if the last book were being written now, the earliest material would have been formed sometime around the seventh century! The writing has different styles, different outlooks, and a very human side to it. Biblical thought itself develops and blossoms throughout those centuries as it moves out of the darkness of near paganism into the shining light of the teaching of Jesus.

And still, despite these many authors who have contributed to our Bible, Christians have always held that there is one Author to it all. The Lord, who works through these many authors, gives to this unusual collection a real unity. In all of Scripture there is one truth unfolding, one message so great that it took thirteen centuries and seventy-three books to tell.

Out of this vast library, I usually choose the short Book of Jonah to start people actually reading the Bible. Among its many qualifications for this position in the course are its brevity, its humour, and its story. Many of the things which the leader wants to say about the book can be said by re-telling the story — which also makes it a reasonably easy book to teach.

Jonah is a satire, which means that it uses exaggeration and humour to get its point across. It was written during a time when the Old Testament people were proud to be Jewish, so proud that they were beginning to despise those who weren't Jewish. This was after they returned from exile in Babylon. The Book of Jonah satirises this exclusivist outlook.

Jonah himself is modelled on an historical character (Cf II Kings 14:25), but the historical Jonah never went through the experiences related in this book. The historical Jonah has the distinction of being one of the few true prophets mentioned in the Old Testament who predicted military success for Israel, instead of the usual warnings; from the snippet in II Kings, we can see that he had a chauvinistic, nationalist side to his character. The author of Jonah takes that and fleshes out for us a nationalistic, small-minded, hard-hearted and unwilling prophet, and sends him with a message to the most godless city on earth: Nineveh.

Nineveh was the opposite of everything God's people stood for. It was the capital of an empire that had devoured the "Ten Lost Tribes" by assimilation. Good prophets delighted in

*Jonah set out in the opposite direction
in order to get away from the Lord.*

predicting its downfall.

When Jonah gets the call, he tries to escape. He takes a boat for Tarshish (in the opposite direction). The famous whale incident is only God's way of getting him back on the job. Jonah hates his task, and doesn't seem to have all that warm a fondness for the Lord who sends him on it. All the way through the book he is cold, hard, bitter and closed.

Now contrast that with the Gentiles in the book. They are always open to God's message, reverent, and repentant. They are the exact opposite to the figure of Jonah. In the last chapter of the book, it is the sinful pagans who have done what God wanted, while Jonah makes it clear that he is firmly opposed to God's working in the world. Yet he is God's chosen, he is God's prophet.

The humour of the book is in the contrasts between pagans and prophet and in the wonderful exaggerations of the storyteller (the "fish story", the description of the size of Nineveh, the speed with which they repent, the misery of Jonah in the last chapter). One point which the book makes is that God loves ALL people, those in Nineveh as well as those in Jerusalem. The book also points out that sometimes God has to work harder to make a prophet repent than he does for a whole city of pagan sinners.

MATERIAL

Jonah 1-4

AIM OF SESSION

To give some idea of the nature and purpose of Scripture, and to open up the message of the Book of Jonah.

SESSION NOTES

Aims of the Group
— to discover the Bible
— all have some knowledge of the Scripture
— all have something to contribute to the group
— to study the Bible as the *Word of God* not just as interesting, ancient writings
— part of a conversation
— the Bible is a means of getting to know God, not just getting to know about him.

The Bible is a Collection of Books
— written in three different languages
— from a wide geographical area
— over at least thirteen hundred years
— different types of writing (poetry, philosophy, stories, folklore, historical writing)
— reflects a variety of outlooks

Despite many authors, Scripture has one author
— one truth
— one message unfolding

TIMES & PLACES 1250 BC—100 AD	PALESTINE GREECE BABYLON ROME

LIBRARY OF BOOKS

LANGUAGES	HEBREW ARAMAIC GREEK

TYPES OF WRITINGS	POETRY PHILOSOPHY HISTORICAL MATERIAL FICTIONAL MATERIAL

The Book of Jonah: Introduction

— a satire, loaded with humour and exaggeration

— written at a time when Jews were excessively nationalistic

— Jews were God's only people

— many felt that God didn't care about any others

— although the story is non-historical, Jonah is based on a prophet who seems to have been himself very nationalistic

— the Jonah of the book is small-minded and unwilling to do what God asks him

— the pagans (Gentiles) in the book are open, reverent and repentant of their sins.

NOTES ON THE TEXT

1:1-3. Jonah is told to go to Nineveh, the great enemy of God's people. He catches a ship bound for the other end of the world, thinking that if he could get away from Israel, he could get away from the Lord.

1:5-6. The pagan sailors immediately start praying when disaster strikes, while Jonah irreligiously sleeps.

1:7-15. Reluctantly, the pagan sailors throw Jonah over — and they pray most piously to Yahweh, Jonah's God.

1:17-2:10. The famous fish enters to bring Jonah back to his starting point. The prayer in the belly of the whale seems to be an old psalm put into the story because of its watery imagery.

3:3. A lovely touch of exaggeration. What city takes three days to get across, even in the Christmas rush hours?

3:4-9. More exaggeration. The pagans take God's message to heart with a vengeance, and even the cattle do penance. If nothing else, this part shows clearly that the story is non-historical, since there would be some evidence if the capital of Assyria "got religious" overnight in the way described.

3:10. God changes his mind. Scripture doesn't usually speak of God in the pure, philosophical ways which we would prefer, but in a very down-to-earth, concrete way. No one really loves a philosophical God, anyway.

4:1-4. Jonah is upset — after all, he's promised all these people that they would be destroyed. Jonah is bitter, and God doesn't argue.

4:5. Jonah watches, just in case the Lord should change his mind again.

4:6-9. Jonah experiences suffering to open his heart; it only makes him angry.

45

4:10-11. The Lord explains why he has to be tender-hearted.

Conclusions

— God loves ALL people, not just Jews (or Christians).
— It can take more to convert a prophet than a city of pagans.

Discussion for this session could be completely open "to the floor".

MATERIAL AND DISCUSSION QUESTIONS
FOR SESSION TWO

The Letter of James 1-2.

— In what ways do we show the type of bias James speaks of in 2:1-9?

— What are some of the characteristics of real Christianity according to James?

Second Session
A Letter from a Jewish Christian

James 1, 2

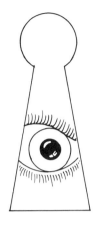

James gives us a glimpse of early Jewish Christianity.

Few books of the New Testament speak so directly to the modern reader as the Letter of James. One wonders why so little use is made of it in the Sunday Lectionary; but that doesn't stop the parish Bible group from taking a closer look at its highly explosive contents.

One of the first questions that you will ask, or have asked, is "Who is James?" This sort of question doesn't come up with a letter by St Paul or with many of the other New Testament books (although, of course, sometimes it should), so studying the Letter of James has the advantage of being able to take an early look at the whole area of biblical authorship, and to do it in context of a book whose authorship has few sentimental attachments for members of the group.

The naive approach takes the view that the author's name on a book means that each and every word flows from his pen (or typewriter or word-processor). Yet most people do acknowledge the existence of people such as ghost-writers and book editors. But apart from this type of qualification, today's standards are rather strict: if someone's name appears on a book who had nothing to do with it, we judge that deception of some degree is intended.

The ancient world was not so strict. The name of a person attached to a piece of writing could, of course, at times indicate the actual author; but other possibilities are present. A name might indicate one of the major sources, one of the key figures behind the contents of the work. This is quite imaginable even in a modern context: if a person wanted to write an article applying the teaching of St Francis of Assisi to modern materialism, drawing on his life and thought, no one could fault the author for entitling the piece, "The Message of St Francis to the Modern World". This is the same kind of association between a work and a key figure which the ancients would have handled by a simple attribution of the work to the key figure.

A third way in which a name becomes attached to a piece of writing in biblical times is as an appeal to the authority of the person, either with real claims as a direct disciple of the person named, or with presumed claims that the contents of the work represent a valid extension of the person's thought. Again, this is quite common in a somewhat different guise in modern publication: today such a work would be entitled "A Freudian Analysis of Certain Drug Induced Hallucinations" or the like. The only major difference between our way of associating names with these types of works and the ancient method is that today we would be certain to attach the real author's name as well.

The simple attachment of a name to biblical books without qualification makes questions of authorship a bit thorny; the result is that sometimes books are thought to be the work of people who didn't write a sentence of them (such as Solomon's association with the Book of Wisdom, for example, which was written in Greek whereas Solomon lived two hundred years before the first written Greek works were ever composed). At the other extreme, no matter what the biblical book, one could find some scholar who would question whether the traditional author had anything to do with it.

All of which brings us back to the Letter of James and its supposed author. It is a question worth asking, for to locate a work in its human surroundings will enrich our understanding of its divine message. Yet our answers to the questions of authorship can never be one hundred per cent certain, only a tentative solution based on the evidence in our possession. And the evidence for James? Well, for one thing, there are four candidates in the New Testament, four men by the name of James. We can safely eliminate one of these before going much further, James, the father of the apostle Jude. That leaves us with two Jameses among the Twelve and also James, the brother of the Lord (see explanation of this term in Session Fourteen, note on Jn 7:3-9.)

47

So what evidence does the letter itself give us? It is extremely Jewish in tone, so much so that Martin Luther didn't really feel that it belonged in the New Testament at all. It also has the tone of a person of high standing in the Church. Now all of the three Jameses aforementioned were Jewish, but the most prominent of these by far is James, the brother of the Lord, who was leader of the Mother Church in Jerusalem (see Acts 15 for some idea of his standing). So I would tend to think that the "James" intended by the title is James, brother of the Lord and leader of the Jerusalem Church.

The next question is harder to answer: was the name of James attached to the work by someone else, or was he, in fact, in some real sense the author? This is complicated by the practice of attaching a name to a book long after it was written, so that at times someone who was not in the original author's mind at all later gets the credit for the book (as is the case with the Letter to the Hebrews and St Paul). The main objection to James actually having written the Letter of James is that it is composed in Greek, and a type of Greek which is clearly not a translation from Aramaic or any other language; the common scholarly opinion is that the native tongue of Jesus and those closely associated with him was Aramaic. However, there is a considerable body of evidence to show that Greek was very widespread in Palestine in our Lord's day, and especially in his own region of Galilee. So perhaps this main objection isn't as insuperable as it was once considered.

If we take the minority opinion and actually say that James is the major force behind the letter, interesting things begin to happen. Since James was the leader of the Jerusalem Church, we have here a work which comes from early Jewish Christianity written for Jewish Christians (one of two in the whole New Testament). James was put to death in 62 AD, so that would make this letter relatively early among the New Testament books. James' teaching on faith and works was long seen as a modification of Paul's message of liberation, but that is based on a date for the Letter of James *after* those of Paul, and in reaction to them. If we place the Letter of James *before* those of Paul, it completely removes the notion of literary confrontation: James is addressing Law abiding Jewish Christians, while Paul is writing to those who are being tempted to adopt the Jewish Law approach to religion. The supposed conflict between James and Paul really disperses when we notice that they mean two different things by faith: for Paul, faith is a commitment of life and deep-seated trust in the Lord; for James, it is intellectual assent to a body of doctrines.

Studying the Letter of James should convince any group that the study of Scripture is not just an intellectual exercise, but an activity which challenges our lives and which prepares us for real Christian growth.

MATERIAL
James 1, 2

AIM OF SESSION

To make some incursion into the area of authorship of biblical books in general and of James in particular; to begin study of the Letter of James.

SESSION NOTES

Problems of Authorship

— today, we accept ghost-writers, editors, etc.

— the ancient world was not so strict. A name attached to a work could indicate:

a) one of the major sources, or figure behind the key sources

b) an appeal to authority
— with real claims, as by a direct disciple

— with presumed claims of someone who feels that he can speak in the name and thought of a great man of the past

c) the actual author

— locating a work in its human setting helps us to appreciate the divine message.

Who is James?

— four candidates in the New Testament

— probably James, brother of the Lord, head of the Jerusalem Church

— the Jerusalem Church was basically composed of Christians of Jewish nationality who kept the Law of Moses

— James himself seems to have been respected by many non-Christian Jews as a devout man, often to be found at prayer in the Temple; known as "James the Just"

— James martyred 62 AD

The Letter Itself

— practical advice, practical Christianity

— a glimpse of early Jewish Christianity; most of the books of the New Testament are written for non-Jewish Christians

— quite possibly a very early piece in the New Testament

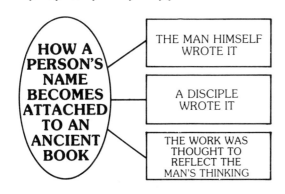

HOW A PERSON'S NAME BECOMES ATTACHED TO AN ANCIENT BOOK

THE MAN HIMSELF WROTE IT

A DISCIPLE WROTE IT

THE WORK WAS THOUGHT TO REFLECT THE MAN'S THINKING

Faith Versus Works

— This topic is important in James, and also in much of Paul

— Luther made this question the most important difference between himself and the Catholicism of his day

— He saw Paul as saying that faith alone brings salvation but the Church as saying that you worked (and bought! — indulgences) your way into heaven

— Luther wanted to cut the Letter of James from the New Testament as a book which contradicted Christian teaching

— Many Christians (especially Evangelicals) still follow Luther's thinking

— There is no contradiction between Paul and James: they simply use the term "faith" in different ways:

  — James means faith as belief

  — Paul means faith as trust in the Lord and commitment to him, not just intellectual assent

— Church teaching *does* teach that we are saved by faith in Paul's sense and definitely not by our own merits, but it is a faith that makes demands on our lives (see Session Nine on Galatians).

NOTES ON THE TEXT

1:1. The twelve tribes were the basic division of Israel, being descended from the twelve sons of Israel (Jacob). James may be using the term to say that he is addressing either the whole of the New Israel (the Church) *or* specifically Jewish Christians.

1:2-4, 12-15. Temptation in the New Testament is not an inclination to do wrong, but an experience which really puts one's faith to the test. It is aptly described as being brought to the brink without going over. In the New Testament world, it often meant facing martyrdom.

1:5. Wisdom in Scripture is not being clever, but knowing the best way to lead your life. The whole of the letter is concerned with wisdom, and more than once, he indicates what is the nature of wisdom. The first thing, in this verse, is that it is a gift of God and not an accomplishment of man.

1:9-11. James demands that we see present conditions of life as transitory, especially the favourable conditions.

1:19-25. More about Wisdom, even though the word is missing. We can see emerging the theme of religion and its effect on one's life. James has a benign attitude towards the Law as a revelation from God (and, of course, he means Law under the type of interpretation in Matt 5 which is also from a Jewish Christian background). Verse 20 on its own could provide fuel for an entire night's discussion. Verses 26-27 centre even more on the nature of authentic Christianity.

2:2. The well-dressed man in the "shining" tunic is thought by many scholars to be a political candidate (from the Latin *candidatus* which referred to the shining white garment they wore).

2:5-7. These verses indicate the social standing of the early Christians of James' circle.

2:8-13. There is more to religion than warm feelings of affection for James, although love indeed sums it all up.

2:14-26. James brings out the cudgels on purely intellectual faith. His argument is at its climax in 2:19-20.

QUESTIONS FOR DISCUSSION

— In what ways do we show the type of bias James speaks of in 2:1-9?

— What are some of the characteristics of real Christianity?

MATERIAL AND DISCUSSION QUESTIONS FOR SESSION THREE

The Letter of James 3-5

— How do the two types of wisdom in Jms 3:13ff influence our decision making?

— Does James exaggerate the influence of the tongue?

Third Session
Spectrum of Scripture
James 3-5

Part of the purpose of this session is to give the participants an indication of how important it is to connect one biblical passage with another. There is an understandable tendency to read a verse or two from the Scripture on a subject and to feel that one can say with confidence on the strength of these verses, "The Bible teaches . . ." It is a practice which can lead one very far astray. The verses of Scripture interplay with each other as they weave their grand tapestry: one passage might modify another, one verse can show how a general saying works out in particular cases (for instance, compare Lk 6:30 with II Thess 3:6-12). More often, a passage in Scripture may be deliberately echoing an older passage, or drawing on the teaching of more than one passage (as in the case of the example used in the session notes). Only after exploring these other passages can the Scripture reader form a picture of what the Bible really does teach about a certain subject.

The principle of consulting related passages will be familiar to anyone who listens to the Sunday Lectionary, for the purpose of the first reading is usually to highlight some aspect of the gospel to be read. A practical example could therefore be found no farther away than next Sunday's readings, though some of these pairings are not as successful as others. All but the most unsatisfactory editions of the Scriptures will have some cross references, and the best set of these in an English language Bible is undoubtedly the *Jerusalem Bible Standard Edition,* and even these are anything but exhaustive (exhausting perhaps for the ordinary reader who attempts to consult each one as he goes along, but not exhaustive).

In short, then, the practice of reading related texts is always going to enrich the reader's understanding of the first passage, and a total neglect of the practice is in danger of misreading the Scriptures. On some subjects, especially the more doctrinal ones, tracing the various texts can give a real sense of the way ideas develop and blossom through the centuries of revelation. A quick idea of this type of development can be got by reading an article on a general topic, such as "death" or "Messiah" in a good reference book of biblical theology.

The Letter of James, coming as it does from a Jewish Christian perspective, is steeped in the Old Testament treasures. Much of it has the tone of the advice of the Wisdom literature, so when we look for parallels, it's the Wisdom literature which will provide the richest ore. The reader should also look for other statements on the same subject within the book under study itself, especially in a longer work such as a gospel — but shorter works like James can also speak on a topic in more than one place.

"The lash of a whip makes a welt, but the lash of a tongue smashes bones!" (Sir 28:17)

The section selected in the session notes for this exercise is Jms 3:1-12 on the danger of the tongue. Other passages in the letter which mention the tongue are Jms 1:26; 4:11-12; 5:12. What James has to say on speech is some of the most thought-provoking material in the book, but it does not exist in a vacuum. The Old Testament Wisdom literature (which is basically concerned with how to live a serene and God fearing life) has much to say about the use and abuse of speech, and it will be an energetic Bible group that will succeed in investigating the handful of references given in the notes!

Use of the Old Testament Wisdom literature leads naturally to the discussion in James on the nature of true wisdom (Jms 3:13f). It should be made clear that biblical wisdom has nothing to do with philosophical speculation; it is more concerned with how to make the best decisions, how to best order one's life. For much of the Old Testament it was thought that living religiously would naturally bring one every happiness and prosperity. Even though the Book of Job was meant to be the tomb and gravemarker for this idea, its grandchildren still live with us: you don't have to travel far to find people who feel that both affliction and prosperity are somehow deserved, and the so-called "work ethic" believes in part that the heavenly bank balance is generally reflected in the earthly one.

But by the time of James, the difference between living the good life in religious terms and in secular terms is at its widest. James can even point to the fact that it is the poor who have responded to God's call while the rich act as the enemies of the gospel (Jms 2:5-6). There are two answers, then, to the question of how to live the good life, depending on whether you consider the good life to be eternal or earth-bound, and for James this means that there are two types of wisdom: one which might get you ahead for the time being, and one which is in line with the good news of Christ.

James also contains a good lesson in scriptural humility (Jms 4), the exact opposite of being proud and demanding. Scriptural humility is acknowledging God's place in human affairs, realising that everything is ultimately under his control. James sees that much of the troubles and strife in any community come from the demanding desires of human hearts taking precedence over everything else (4:1-6). The Christian attitude is that all plans and even life itself depend on the Lord allowing them (4:13-15).

The Second Coming (*parousia* in Greek) enters into the Letter of James, as it does into many New Testament letters. In contrast to the morbid way in which many Christians think of the end of the world, James speaks with expectancy and eagerness for this great event; whereas today many look at the Second Coming with fear because they think of it as the Last Judgement, the early Christian saw it as the day when the promises of Christ would reach their fulfilment as he came with reward and blessings for his faithful ones. In recent years, more of this New Testament attitude has been spread through the revised Advent liturgies.

Few will miss the reference to anointing in 5:14, but not many will know that olive oil was a common medicine in New Testament times (see *Lk 10:34*). Oil for the sick continues the type of common symbol found in sacramental practice with bread for eating and wine for drinking and the waters of rebirth. The confession of sins in *5:16* is not sacramental confession, of course, but in the same line of thinking that sin is not just something between me and the Lord but something which affects others as well. The most important passage concerning our practice of the Sacrament of Reconciliation is, of course, Jn 20:22-23; but this passage in James is far from irrelevant.

MATERIAL

James 3-5

AIM OF SESSION

To give some experience of the way that texts in Scripture combine with each other and relate to each other to enrich the reader's awareness of total biblical teaching on a subject; to conclude the study of the Letter of James.

SESSION NOTES

The Importance of Cross References

There is an inclination to read a passage and to say on the strength of that one text, "The Bible teaches . . ." Not that simple; no biblical passage exists in isolation

— the principle of the First Reading in the Sunday Lectionary is to use an Old Testament passage to highlight something in the gospel reading

— one passage often acts as the key which opens another passage (e.g. Lk 11:29-32 and the Book of Jonah)

— sometimes a text clarifies another, sometimes even corrects it (see Mt 5:21-48)

— investigation of some related passages will ALWAYS enrich the understanding of the text being studied.

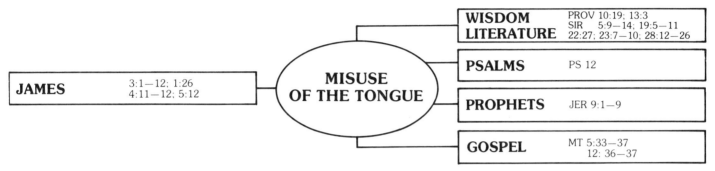

| JAMES | 3:1—12; 1:26
4:11—12; 5:12 |

MISUSE OF THE TONGUE

WISDOM LITERATURE	PROV 10:19; 13:3 SIR 5:9—14; 19:5—11 22:27; 23:7—10; 28:12—26
PSALMS	PS 12
PROPHETS	JER 9:1—9
GOSPEL	MT 5:33—37 12: 36—37

An Exercise in Cross References: Jms 3:1-12, The Tongue

A few points made in this section:

— the tongue is powerful for its size, can take over a person

— the tongue has great destructive power (3:5b-8)

— the tongue is the organ of hypocrisy (3:9-12)

There are other references to the misuse of speech in James: other places in the same work give the most important cross references.

— Jms 1:26 Control of speech a criterion for true religion.

— Jms 4:11-12 Useless criticism infringes the rights of God.

— Jms 5:12 Christian speech needs no oath to back it up.

Texts from the Wisdom Literature

— Proverbs 10:19; 13:3 Too much talk is dangerous.

— Sirach 5:9-14 Better to be silent than quick to speak (see also James 1:19).

— Sirach 19:5-11 The value of keeping confidences, with powerful imagery in verses 10-12.

— Sirach 22:27 Even the desire to control the tongue doesn't always produce the goods.

— Sirach 23:7-10 The high regard for the divine name Yahweh lies behind these verses.

— Sirach 28:12-26 Some very close echoes to what James says on the tongue.

A Sample Text from the Prophets

— Jeremiah 9:1-9 The unfaithfulness of the people shows itself in hypocritical speech, which God will punish.

A Sample Text from the Psalms

— Psalm 12 The dishonest speech of the wicked is contrasted with the trustworthy Word of the Lord.

Two Texts from the Gospel

— Mt 5:33-37 The unnecessity of oaths.

— Mt 12:36-37 Useless words lead to judgement.

Conclusion

After investigation of parallel texts, we have a fuller idea of what James was saying about speech, and are in a better position to say what the Bible teaches about the use of the tongue.

NOTES ON THE TEXT

3:13-18. Wisdom in the Bible is the best way to arrange your life. James sees that there are two possible approaches to this: one spiritual (the wisdom from above; see Jms 1:5), and the materialistic wisdom (the earthly wisdom). He talks briefly about the fruits of each.

4:1-4. Uncontrolled desires eventually make everyone miserable; a worldly way of thinking declares war on God.

4:13-16. True humility (see above, 4:7-10) means knowing that all things are in God's hands.

5:1-6. James is speaking to rich people, but there are probably few in the congregation to hear him (see 2:1-7). He is really addressing the oppressed, telling them that the inequality of society will be set right. He presumes that riches are only had by the exploitation of the less well off (5:4) and implies that luxury can only be had by ignoring the needs of others (5:4-5). Is his view still valid? In any event, he clearly implies that riches are not a security, but a danger on Judgement Day (5:3).

5:7-8. The Second Coming is something to be looked forward to, not dreaded. Most of the New Testament books make some reference to this day when all the promises of the Lord will be fulfilled, and God's faithful people rewarded.

5:14. Olive oil was a common medicine, used for dressing sores and wounds, and even taken internally; but this is not a performance of first-aid. It is clearly a prayer by the presbyters (from which we get our English word "priest") for healing, the Sacrament of the Sick.

QUESTIONS FOR DISCUSSION

— How do the two types of wisdom in Jms 3:13ff influence our decision making?

— Does James exaggerate the influence of the tongue?

MATERIAL AND DISCUSSION QUESTIONS FOR SESSION FOUR

Exodus 19-20, 24

— What does the term "Covenant" mean in modern ears?

— In what way does Jesus continue the idea of covenant relationship between God and Christians?

(It would be worth mentioning that the reading material, together with chapters 21-23, gives the basic story of the covenant making event in the Old Testament. Although there are a few covenants in the Old Testament, it is this covenant at Sinai which was seen as the most important of them all.)

Fourth Session
Covenant

Exodus 19-20, 24

If participation in a Bible group does no more for people than give them a slight understanding of covenant, then the whole venture is worthwhile. With this session, they dive into the depths of biblical waters, exploring the most basic idea which holds the Bible together. Exploration of this idea should also show that knowledge of the cultural background of Scripture is vital for understanding God's Word.

"Covenant" is a technical term in today's world, no matter what way you approach it. For example, in the world of fund raising it refers to a special tax-free way of giving to charity. Religiously, it is a word which people hear at every celebration of the Eucharist, and which floats meaninglessly in and out of their ears.

Not so in the biblical world. In the Ancient Near East, covenants were part of daily life and commerce. Whenever any matter was to be acted upon — from water rights to an international cease-fire — the agreement was sealed by a covenant. So when Yahweh used covenant as a way of binding himself to his people, he was speaking their language. He took something familiar to them in secular life and made it sacred.

The development of covenant form and thought is a complicated area. It might be helpful to imagine an early stage in its development to highlight the logic and basic structure of covenant. Covenant could be called "a way of sealing pre-literate agreements". For example, Ishmael and I have a dispute over water rights to a well on the boundary of our adjoining fields. Finally, we reach an agreement that we use the well on alternating days of the week; but how do we seal that agreement? Written agreements are useless, since neither Ishmael nor I can read or write. We could make a verbal agreement, but we want something formal and binding. So we call the gods to witness our agreement and to punish the party who breaks it, often by killing an animal or two as a sign of what will happen to the covenant breaker. This simple but dramatic form of covenant is God's way of reassuring Abraham about his promises in Genesis 15.

Apart from the rather vivid curse, covenant had another

The Indian Chief and the big white hero become blood brothers.

guarantee that the condition would be kept: when two people entered covenant, they entered a special type of relationship with each other, bringing each other into their intimate circle of family and friends. A close equivalent from the Holywood westerns is when the Indian Chief and the Big White Hero become blood brothers; they voluntarily enter a relationship which they consider to be as binding as any family bonds. More about this later.

The covenant form developed from such simple beginnings, as we know from the copies of covenant agreements which survive. These covenants are usually between two parties, one in a superior position to the other. Because of this, they are sometimes called suzerainty treaties. They tend to follow a general pattern, although they do not contain all of the elements.

The first element in this pattern is the preamble which lists the titles of the stronger party in the covenant. Since these are full lists of all the royal titles, they can be rather pompous and tedious. In Exodus, the preamble is short and simple: "I am Yahweh your God."

The second element is the historical introduction which lists the history which culminates in this covenant being made. It might, for instance, tell how the fathers of the two covenanting monarchs had certain understandings, or how the superior party came to the rescue of the lesser. Again, in Exodus, this section is concise: "I brought you out of the land of Egypt, the house of slavery."

The heart of the matter is reached in the third element, the prohibitions and demands of the covenant. Since a vital part of covenant is agreement, and since agreements are always about something, this section is essential, and occupies the longest part of the Exodus account of the covenant.

The memorial copy of the covenant could take a few different forms. It might be an actual copy of the wording of the agreement, or a stone erected as a monument to commemorate the event (see Ex 24:4). In practice, the people were reminded of the covenant in several ways: by the Passover celebration, by the traditional formulations which carried the covenant conditions, in covenant renewal ceremonies, by the Ark of the Covenant, and so on.

One element of the usual covenant pattern would be unthinkable in the Old Testament: the calling of divine witnesses to oversee the carrying out of the covenant. You couldn't really imagine Yahweh calling on Baal and Molech to witness Israel's agreement to these conditions! Of course, the usual role of the gods was not to make covenants, but to oversee them, which is what makes the biblical notion of covenant such an exciting insight into the way God works with his people. Nevertheless, there are times when we get the feeling that the whole universe plays witness to the covenant on Sinai and to the breaking of it (as, for instance, in the opening verses of the book of Isaiah or in Psalm 50.)

The concluding element in the pattern is the blessing and curse, a blessing for those who keep the covenant and a curse for those who break it. Blessings and curses were thought of as being much more efficacious in those times than now. The covenant partners hung these blessings and curses over their own heads, suspended by the conditions of the covenant, ready to drop when the covenant would be fulfilled or broken. Their modern descendant is the statement of the "May God strike me dead if . . ." variety. A taste of these in Exodus is provided in Ex 23:20-28, but, for a richer sampling, try Deut 28.

When a modern reader first encounters Ex 19-24, the one thing which will strike him is that it is full of laws, and his Christian heritage will make him revolt a bit against this approach to religion. One must be careful not to paint the Torah with the legalistic approach of hundreds of years later. In context, these laws are conditions of the relationship. It might be well to point out that every relationship is conditioned in varied implicit and explicit ways. Much more important than the conditions is the relationship itself.

The covenant relationship flows in two directions, with specific expectations from both sides. Yahweh promises love, loving kindness *(ḥesed)*, and faithfulness *('emeth)*; from his people, Yahweh can expect love and faithfulness *('emeth)*. In fact, *hesed* and *'emeth* make a good summary of the covenant relationship. *Hesed* is a tender, almost excessively benign predisposition toward someone, while *'emeth* is true blue loyalty and complete dependability. These Hebrew words still contain the kernel of the Christian's relationship with God through Jesus Christ, and may well lie behind such familiar New Testament words as grace, truth, faith and love — at least in some of their uses.

One thing that might be noted about the various laws in this section of Exodus: they seem to either defend the position of Yahweh (by prohibiting other cults and pagan religious practices) or to ensure the rights and dignity of the Israelites. Another point worth mentioning is that not all of these laws are new with Moses, as we discovered when we found many of them in the famous Code of Hammurabi which pre-dates Sinai by five hundred years.

A special note on the *lex talionis* (Ex 21:23-24), which is an echo from the Code of Hammurabi: when it is invoked today, it is often intended as a license for vengeance. That is far from its original intention. Its first purpose was to limit vengeance, not to allow it, to prevent the removal of the whole lower jawbone in reprisal for one tooth. Christ continues the work of these verses in Mt 5:38-42.

One can hardly mention covenant without mentioning the special significance of blood. In the Scriptures, blood is a sign for life, at times almost equating life (in the same way that we associate life and breath, perhaps). Blood becomes a covenant element on two levels. First, as significance of the curse which the parties invoke: the scene in Gen 15 would entail a lot of blood in this sense. The second level is what we have in Ex 24 and in the Eucharist: the one blood spilt on the people and on the altar (representing Yahweh) stood for the one life that now exists between God and his people as covenant partners.

The group will have to refer to the ideas in this session again and again, so the leader should not expect that they all go down smoothly at the first gulp. This session earns its position at the start of the series, not because the central concept is easy, but because it is important.

Some of the material in the Torah is older than Moses

AIM OF SESSION

To introduce the central concept of covenant, and to show the relevance of some knowledge of the background of the time in understanding the Word of God.

SESSION NOTES

The Importance of Background

— covenant, today, is a word which has little everyday meaning

— it must be looked at in the everyday life of biblical times

— this is true of many things in Scripture: one must always look to see the significance of even everyday things in the biblical world (e.g. water, light, pigs, etc.)

The Simple Basics of Covenant

— in an illiterate society, how does one formalise agreements?

— covenant: the way to seal the pre-literate agreements

— condition of agreement

— under oath, blessing and curse.

— the covenant created a permanent relationship between the partners (like the blood-brother relationship of the Westerns).

57

```
┌─────────────────────────────────────────────┐
│              FORMAL COVENANT                  │
│  1 PREAMBLE WITH TITLES    4 THE MEMORIAL     │
│  2 HISTORICAL PROLOGUE     5 GODS WHO ARE WITNESSES │
│  3 PROHIBITIONS & DEMANDS  6 BLESSING & CURSE │
└─────────────────────────────────────────────┘
```

```
┌──────────────────────────┐        ╭─────────────╮        ┌──────────────────────┐
│       RELATIONSHIP       │        │             │        │     AGREEMENT        │
│          LOVE            │────────│  COVENANT   │────────│                      │
│  LOVING KINDNESS (HESED) │        │             │        │    CONDITIONS        │
│  FAITHFULNESS  ('EMETH)  │        ╰─────────────╯        │  BLESSING & CURSES   │
└──────────────────────────┘                              └──────────────────────┘
```

— Gen 15 presents the covenant between Yahweh and Abraham in these terms, the dead animals representing the curse.

The Developed Form of Covenant (between unequal partners)

— Preamble with Titles (Ex 20:2a)

— Historical Introduction (Ex 20:2b)

— Prohibitions and Demands (Ex 20:3-23:18)

— The Memorial (Ex 24:4)

— Gods who are Witnesses (not in Exodus)

— Blessing and Curse (Ex 23:20-28)

Laws as Conditions of the Relationship

— Yahweh's side of the relationship:

   — love

   — loving kindness *(hesed)*

   — faithfulness *('emeth)*
      (this is the ironic complaint of Jonah in Jon 4:1-2!)

— Israel's side of the relationship:

   — love

   — faithfulness to Yahweh, and to his laws.

Two guiding principles for individual laws:

— no god but Yahweh and no cultic practices but his

— the rights and dignity of the Israelite must be protected

— some of the material in the Torah is older than Moses
   (Code of Hammurabi 17th/18th century BC).

NOTES ON THE TEXT

19:1. The people of Israel had escaped, but far from being a nation, they had no land, no law, and little unity. The covenant would be the means of making them a nation.

19:3-6. Yahweh, as the more important party, proposes a covenant.

19:13-16. After the people accept the invitation, preparations are made. Mt Sinai is to be treated as especially holy, since it is the place of the solemn theophany. Ancient Israelites believed that casual or uninvited contact with the holy (such as the gazing upon God) would mean tragedy and usually death. The theophany begins in verses 17-19.

19:20-25. A second account of the above section. The first four books of the Pentateuch were written from a few different sources, so often episodes are repeated from different viewpoints, sometimes giving a modern reader the impression of different incidents in a continuous story.

20:1-17. The Ten Commandments (Decalogue), which are the beginning of the formal covenant form. Verse 7 eventually led to the near total avoidance of the use of the divine name Yahweh by the time of Christ, and most modern translations substitute Lord (for the Hebrew 'adonai) in the Old Testament whenever the name Yahweh occurs. Notice, too, that the basic command in verses 8-11 is to rest (sabbath being the Hebrew word for rest).

21:23-24. The *lex talionis*, a restriction on vengeance, not a licence for vendettas.

22:26-27 The welfare of the poor is safeguarded even against the demands of the strictest justice.

23:2 Integrity is required even in spite of "majority rule".

23:10-11 Even the fields get a rest! The idea is that the sabbath means doing what you want to; if the fields wish to sprout weeds and such along with the self-seeding produce, that's their business.

23:19b This seemingly trite prohibition was against a pagan Canaanite practice. Orthodox Jews will not eat meat and milk produce at the same meal because of a very strict interpretation of it.

23:20-26 The blessing in store for the people who keep the covenant.

24:1-3 The people agree to the terms of the covenant.

24:4-8 Moses makes a copy of the agreement and conducts a ratifying ceremony. The blood symbolises the common life between Yahweh and his people.

24:9-11 The leaders of Israel conclude the covenant with a sacrificial meal in the presence of Yahweh. The Eucharist is also a sacrificial meal which celebrates a covenant.

QUESTIONS FOR DISCUSSION

— What does the term "Covenant" mean in modern ears?

— In what way does Jesus continue the idea of a covenant relationship between God and Christians?

MATERIAL AND DISCUSSION QUESTIONS FOR SESSION FIVE

Deuteronomy 5-11

— This material shows how basic God was to the Old Testament awareness of Israel's nationhood. Many people will know that the people of Jesus' time expected a great political leader for a Messiah. Does this ancient idea of nationhood throw any light of what the term "Kingdom of God" means in the ears of Jesus' audience?

— To what "nation" does the Christian owe primary allegiance?

Fifth Session
God and Nationhood
Deuteronomy 5-11

The modern religious mentality is truly international, and none of the great religions of mankind are daunted by national boundaries. This makes the Old Testament idea of the relationship between religion and nationality unfamiliar territory to the modern reader. To be sure, the Bible does have a truly international outlook, and one that begins in the pages of the Old Testament; yet the earlier sections of the Old Testament would definitely give the impression that God is the exclusive possession of one nation, and it's hard luck to everyone else.

In the ancient Near East, gods did belong to nations. Two of the most important aspects of primitive religion emphasise important aspects of the state's well-being: fertility and military strength. Each nation had its own pantheon, its own set of divinities, whose special concern was the success of the nation. Our idea of only one real deity would have made little sense to the ancients. The Ra-Amon worshipping Egyptian, for instance, would never have prayed to Marduk, the god of Babylon; but neither would he have questioned Marduk's existence. Marduk existed alright according to the Egyptian's mentality; he just didn't have any concern about Egyptians. Nor would the Egyptian have ever thought of converting a Babylonian to worship of Ra-Amon. He would have simply said, "Each nation has its gods and that's the way it should be. Ra-Amon is the most powerful of all gods, and that is why Egypt is the great nation that it is."

This close connection between religion and nation meant that there was absolutely no separation of Church and State; in fact, in many ways the two were identical. This gave the king a special place in the hierarchy, a type of chief priest above all others. Since he ruled the people in the name of the god, he was also considered to be in a special relationship to the realm of the divine: in Egypt he was an incarnate god, in other places a son of the deity. Even in Israel, the coronation song tells the new king that Yahweh has begotten him on the day of coronation *(Ps 2:7)*. In Israel, however, the king was as subject to Yahweh's decrees as anyone else, and could be rejected by Yahweh, as happened in the case of Saul.

Each earthly battleground was a reflection of a heavenly struggle

The nation worshipped the gods for the preservation of the state. The gods were the nation's security, and if things were right in heaven, everything would be fine within the boundaries. The enemies of the state were, naturally, the enemies of the gods; so the national deities were expected to do battle, conquering invading armies and other threats to the national existence. Echoes of this can be heard in the prayers of Israel as well, and Psalm 2 also serves as an example of this.

The ancient Near Eastern gods had to be warriors to do their job. Each earthly battleground was a reflection of a heavenly struggle, and the victor in heaven determined who would win on earth. This popular image of the gods battling in the heavens over the destinies of man never reaches the pages of the Old Testament in a very crude form. The one exception is Daniel 10:12-21 which speaks about a heavenly struggle between the forces of Yahweh and the guardian spirits of Persia and Javan which are to determine the fortunes of Israel. This popular mentality did cause grave problems at one stage in Old Testament history, however: when Babylon's armies conquered Judah, the haunting question troubled many Jewish minds, "Does this mean that Marduk, god of Babylon, had overcome Yahweh?" This theological crisis did much to bring about the realisation that Yahweh was not just the only God for Israel: he is, in fact, the only true God for anybody. Other gods are simply spirits in rebellion against his sovereign rule.

Law, too, has a numinous aura in this ancient Near Eastern outlook. The Law comes to the people from the deity to the king. The stele on which the Code of Hammurabi is inscribed (see Session Four) has at the top a picture of King Hammurabi receiving the law from his god. There could be no difference between civil law and religious law, and we see the two intertwined without distinction in the Old Testament.

Israel began with this same general pattern of thought, although in Israel it received a unique development which makes it nearly unrecognisable at the New Testament end of the process. The Pentateuch shows that Israel was aware that its existence was completely the action of Yahweh. Israel was made into a nation by covenant with the Lord; when they came out of Egypt, they were no people but a band of escaping Semites. It was at Sinai in the biblical perspective that they became a nation, with Yahweh as their Head of State. Israel was not alone in its divine leadership, for all nations were (in theory) theocracies.

Deuteronomy provides an interesting example of this outlook. The history of Deuteronomy's composition is too complex to allow for more than the vaguest notion of it to be given here. II Kings 22:8-13 tells the story of its discovery in the reign of Josiah, the reforming king of Judah. It acted as a

REFORMING CONSTITUTION for a people who had corrupted greatly the spirit and practice of Yahwistic religion, and it emphasised how basic the Law of God was to the very existence of the state. Deuteronomy takes the format of the last sermons of Moses as Israel is on the brink of the Promised Land, all of which is laced with the blessing/curse aspect of covenant thinking: if you keep these laws, you will live; if you abandon these laws, you will die. Laws in Deuteronomy are not legalism, but principles which are to be made part of the Israelite, expressions of his love and faithfulness *('emeth)* to the God with whom he has made covenant. The Hebrew word which we translate as "law" *(torah)* is much more gentle, meaning "instruction".

A word is in order about monotheism, that contemporary notion of there being only one God which we take so much for granted. The monotheism of Deuteronomy is more qualified than that, of course: it simply holds that there is only one God *for Israel;* other gods might exist, but Israel was to have absolutely nothing to do with them. Even in the New Testament we find that false gods are granted existence, but as demons (I Cor 10:19-21).

Monotheism in the ancient world had another connotation which we miss; to illustrate, I will take a simplified Roman example. If an ancient Roman wanted to be a successful thief, he would be very devoted to the god Mercury, who was the god of thieves, and Mercury would help his career. If his neighbour wanted to have an illicit love affair, he would sacrifice to Venus who would smile down on his endeavour, since that sort of thing was her speciality. But if the thief should stumble into the temple of Venus, he would know that his prayers would only provoke the godess's anger (after all, a lady has some principles!) The lesson is clearly that different gods in the pantheon allow a certain latitude in morality. One God means one morality, and no exceptions. Pluralism of religion would undermine the morality and the political unity of Israel.

The Old Testament also has a much stronger sense of the unity of the nation than would be possible for us. Part of the outlook was biological: a man lived on in his descendants; put the other way around, all the descendants of a man are that person alive today. Even though Israel absorbed unrelated people into its ranks throughout the years, in theory, the whole people remain the descendants of one man, Jacob, whose other name is Israel. In Old Testament thinking, the whole nation can be considered one person, and at times is treated and addressed as such. Nor does the unity of the nation know any distinction of time: what happens to Israel in one age affects its whole history, and the Law accepted at Sinai is accepted by all generations. This way of looking at Israel has been termed CORPORATE PERSONALITY, and its New Testament descendant is the Pauline doctrine of the Body of Christ.

As in the case of covenant, we are treating a subject which is not easy, but basic to an intelligent reading of Scripture. The ancient view of God and nationhood tells the readers why first-century Jews wanted a political Messiah, and why religious zeal often meant terrorism against the Roman occupation forces. It sheds light on why the early books (and parts of the later ones) can seem so bloodthirsty: the enemies of Israel were the irreconcilable enemies of Yahweh, and, as such, deserved what they got. Most important, here one can see how God begins with people where he finds them, and gradually leads them on to where he wants them, to the idea of a New People without racial boundaries, whose obligation it is to spread the invitation to everyone to join its ranks as God's special domain.

MATERIAL

Deuteronomy 5-11

AIM OF SESSION

To convey the common ground between the ancient concepts of religion and nationhood and to demonstrate some of the implications for biblical thinking.

SESSION NOTES

The Ancient Near Eastern Religious Outlook

— today's great religions are international; in the ancient world, gods belonged to particular nations

— the concerns of primitive "gods" were primary concerns of the nation, such as fertility and military strength

— the gods were worshipped for the preservation of the state:

  — the gods secure the state if properly worshipped

  — the gods are warriors on behalf of the state, fighting both earthly and heavenly enemies

  — the state's enemies are automatically enemies of the god

— there is a special relationship between the deity and the king: he is a meeting point between the nation and the realm of the divine

— the law of the land is sacred to the god of the land, coming from him through the authorities of the state:

  — no distinction between religious and civil law

  — the curse of the god rests on the lawbreaker

| THE KING | WAS THE MEETING POINT BETWEEN GOD AND THE NATION |
| THE LAW | WAS GIVEN BY THE GOD THROUGH THE KING |

THE GOD CONCERNED WITH — DEFENCE SECURITY

THE RELATIONSHIP OF DEITY & NATION

God and Nationhood in Ancient Israel

— the very existence of the nation depends on the Covenant with Yahweh; before that, no nation at all

— Israel (like other nations of the time) was a theocracy, with God as its theoretical Head of State and Head of Government

— national existence itself was seen to depend on the observance of the Law

— as in modern mentality, law is seen as the backbone of justice, peace and order in society

— in theological terms, if society were negligent of the Law, Yahweh would not allow that society to continue (see Dt 5:28-33 where moral rectitude and being allowed to inhabit the land are clearly linked)

— in this context, Israel having only one God (Monotheism) had implications which can be missed:

— many gods could mean differing standards of morality; Israel's one God meant that there was one unwavering morality

— pagan pantheons often reflected the rivalries of different localities within the nation (local patron deities echoing the earthly rivalry on a celestial plane); one deity meant that local rivalries could not be lifted to the same supernatural dimension. One deity strengthens national unity

— worship of other gods was a threat to national unity and existence; it showed a weakening of allegiance and of a sense of national identity

The Book of Deuteronomy

— written for a people who had forgotten their religious commitment and identity by someone keenly aware of the danger in which this placed them. (Commonly agreed to come from the Northern Kingdom before the time of its fall, 721 BC. Some of the material is older, of course, and was tailored to local needs after its discovery in the Jerusalem Temple)

— meant as a REFORMING CONSTITUTION to give people a renewed sense of what they as a people were meant to be

— discovered during a religious reform in Jerusalem under King Josiah (640-609 BC). This discovery and its effects are to be found in II Kings 22:8-13

— the basic form of the book is a series of speeches put into the mouth of Moses when the people are about to take possession of the Promised Land

— the nation is addressed in the singular, not "Ye" but "Thou"

— all the people are one person since they come from one forefather, Israel (also called Jacob)

— this also is used to stress the continuity between the conquering ancestors moving into Palestine and the present-day audience of the author

63

— notice the emphasis on everything happening for the generation being addressed in Dt 5:2; 11:2-8

— this is the same mentality as is involved in the yearly Passover celebration: the Exodus not only involved long-gone generations, but the very people seated around the Passover meal this night

— this awareness of the unity of the whole people is called Corporate Personality

— in Deuteronomy, the laws are principles to be made part of one's whole way of thinking and acting (Dt 10:12-13, 16). *Torah,* the Hebrew word which is usually translated "law", has this more general sense of "instruction", "guidance"

  — keeping the commandments is the expression of covenant faithfulness *('emeth)* as part of man's response to God

  — faithfulness is rooted in a sense of dependance upon Yahweh's goodness (Dt 8:6-20)

  — Yahweh's goodness is a free gift, unearned by those who receive it (Dt 9:4-6)

NOTES ON THE TEXT

5:2-3 The covenant at Horeb is something in which all Israelites participate. These words would never have had the effect of making the hearers of later generations think, "Oh, this has nothing to do with us." The notion of corporate personality made them aware of how immediate the ancient covenant was for the present moment.

5:6-21 The essence of the covenant in the form of the Decalogue is repeated.

6:4-9 At least the first verse of this section would have been repeated twice daily by every devout Jew, including Jesus, in the first century. It expresses the fundamental belief of Judaism, and remains for many Jews the most emotive verse in the whole Bible, and the last words on the lips of many dying Israelites. It is, of course, the belief in the unity of God: "Listen, Israel, Yahweh our God, Yahweh is One." The rest of the passage implores the hearer to let the words of the Law be in every thought, word and act.

6:20-25 In the thought of Deuteronomy, keeping the Law meant happiness and prosperity, because it would mean God's blessing. This must be modified by the later thinking of the Book of Job, which shows that suffering is not always the result of an evil life, and by the New Testament teaching on the cross.

7:1-6 The ruthless attitude to the pagans is not one with which the Christian should agree; but perhaps it is more intelligible as trying to prevent paganism creeping into the pure worship of Yahweh. Perhaps the passage is hindsight: the religion of the people was not pure, and this was blamed on the non-eradication of the former inhabitants of the land.

8:7-20 Even blessings can be snares. "Forgetting" is the great tragedy of the author's time: his people have forgotten God.

9:7-19 The philosophical questions about how prayer works will find little sympathy in the Old Testament. Its approach is the picture of a deity who actually changes his mind. This incident has a more attractive telling in Numbers 14.

10:1-5 The Ark of the Covenant was a sign of the presence of Yahweh, perhaps as a tangible footstool to his intangible majesty. It would later be the central cult-item in the Jerusalem Temple.

11:8-17 An explicit linking of the fortunes and existence of the nation with the keeping of the commandments.

QUESTIONS FOR DISCUSSION

— This material shows how basic God was to the Old Testament awareness of Israel's nationhood. Many people will know that the people of Jesus' time expected a great political leader for a Messiah. Does this ancient idea of nationhood throw any light on what the term "Kingdom of God" means in the ears of Jesus' audience?

— To what "nation" does the Christian owe primary allegiance?

MATERIAL AND DISCUSSION QUESTIONS FOR SESSION SIX

Jeremiah 1,4-5

— What part does Jeremiah see God as playing in the current affairs of his time?

— What assurances does God give Jeremiah when he calls him to become a prophet? Does Jeremiah seem eager to say yes?

A First Look at Prophecy

Jeremiah 1, 4-5

The prophetic writings take up nearly a third of the Old Testament, and yet few people have a clear understanding of what biblical prophecy is. To the man in the street, prophecy means looking into the future, seeing how events will turn out, more of a psychic phenomenon than a religious one. For the Bible student, the word takes its meaning from its Greek roots: *phetes*, meaning speaker, and *pro* meaning (in this case) on behalf of. "Prophet" is a religious term for a spokesperson, someone who speaks on behalf of God and who speaks in his name. So the classical Hebrew way of classifying prophets is much wider than our usual way of thinking of prophecy: the great leaders of Israel are written up in the books called "The Earlier Prophets": all those who speak and lead in God's name share in the gift of prophecy.

The people called prophets (in the sense of those who speak oracles) also cover a wide spectrum: Moses is not only a prophet, but according to the Book of Deuteronomy, is the greatest of the prophets (see Dt 18:17ff); there were also charismatic groups who were rather more carried away with ecstasy than modern charismatics would ever think of being (the Old Testament can view this type with a hint of humour, as in I Sam 19:18-24); another type of early prophet are a type of spiritual "yes-men" at court, and this group comes closest to the notion of prophet as seer (an interesting glimpse into their activity is found in I Kings 22:1-28.) But those we usually think of as prophets are the ones whose names are connected with

The popular idea of prophecy is not quite what the Bible had in mind.

the prophetic literature; the Jews call these "the Later Prophets" and scholars refer to them as "the Writing Prophets". Their function was not to gaze into the future, but into the present, to interpret what was happening around them in light of the Word of God. From the evidence, it would seem that some of their message came through extraordinary visions — or at least that was the only way that the prophets could conceive of communicating the experience (see Isaiah 6 or Ezechiel 1, for example). But we should not imagine that this was the normal means for the oracle to come to the prophet; the writings provide much evidence that an internal type of inspiration is at work, triggered by a word or scene perhaps, characterised by a profound certainty that what they are to speak is the message of Yahweh, and not just their own thinking.

The phrase "Writing Prophets" might conjure up the image of Isaiah typing quickly to meet his publisher's deadline, or Hosea autographing scrolls in the Temple courts. The composition of the prophetic books is more complex than that; many hands and many years might be involved. Three areas of writing which can be found in many of the prophetic books are: *oracles* of the prophet himself, usually given in poetry (for easy memorisation) but sometimes given in prose; *biographical material* which gives something of the prophet's setting and career, especially the call he received from Yahweh to prophesy; *continuation* of the prophet's work through his disciples. This last causes the problems, although sometimes the continuation is fairly easily distinguished from the original prophet's work (as in the case of Isaiah 40-66), but sometimes the later writing is intermingled with the original oracles. I think that Bible groups can leave these problems for those who are paid to worry about them.

Biblical prophets were never seen as mystical visionaries, whose prophetic experiences were for their own spiritual edification and consolation. Prophecy puts the prophet into a unique position, of course, but one which is built upon his membership of the covenant people. The prophets are the ones who made tangible the demands of the covenant to Israel, and who insisted that the covenant with Yahweh was the only key to Israel's prospects. The prophets can only be understood if it is remembered that they are speaking first and foremost to the people of their own time about what is happening in their own time. When they speak of the future, it is as a consequence of the present, not as some immutable destiny. The whole point of preaching future destruction is to bring present repentance and to change the future. Remember Jonah?

Since prophets spoke in and about their own times, it is essential to locate them in time and place. Jeremiah is relatively easy to compose a file on: he is of good stock, a priestly family, a young man at the time of his call, and someone who really didn't want the job — either when he was offered it or as he performed his task. Considering both his hesitancy and the misfortunes which were to befall him, Jeremiah might also be credited with much foresight.

The history of his times is also a consideration. The opening of the book tells us that he was called in the reign of Josiah. Now since Josiah was a religious reformer, it must have seemed a good time to be a prophet; but a reforming king does not necessarily mean a reformed people. Politically, Judah had an uneasy pact with Assyria and Egypt, but Babylon was the ascending power and it was making its presence felt more and more. The new king, Jehoiakim, was pompous if not oblivious to the delicate situation the nation was in; in the midst of desperation, Jehoiakim was building palaces. This was to be one of the hardest things which Jeremiah faced: from King Jehoiakim down through officials and priests and the whole hierarchy of the *status quo,* no one wanted to hear what Jeremiah was proclaiming. With the prophet, the whole nation was balanced on a knife edge; with the ruling classes, it was business as usual.

The writing of Jeremiah make a good beginning into prophecy because they throb with the prophet's personality. His oracles are framed by his sense of urgency, because he knows that Judah is now facing its last chance for survival. No one reading these three chapters could feel that Jeremiah's first task was to predict the Messiah; Jeremiah, as prophet, is too concerned with current affairs to give much thought to the far distant future. And his concern was well-founded: his beloved city was destroyed in 587 BC as Jeremiah still exercised his unhappy role to his unbelieving people.

MATERIAL

Jeremiah 1,4,5

AIM OF SESSION

To introduce biblical prophecy in general and the figure of Jeremiah in particular.

SESSION NOTES

The Nature of Prophecy

— biblical prophecy is not an occult art concerned primarily with gazing into the future

— "Prophet" comes from the Greek roots *pro* "on behalf of" and *phetes* "speaker"; a good synonym for "prophet" in the biblical context is "spokesperson"

— the Old Testament knows different types of prophets:

  — Moses, the most important Old Testament spokesman for Yahweh

  — gangs of charismatic ecstatic figures, seen in the books of Samuel and Kings

  — court seers, who were expected to give divine consent to royal designs (cf. I Kings 22)

— the Writing Prophets

— the primary task of the prophet was to interpret contemporary events in the light of the covenant; sometimes this involved saying where things were leading, especially according to the covenant blessings and curses

— although there is evidence that sometimes the prophetic message came to the prophet through visions, more often we should visualise the inspiration as internal, triggered by something which the prophet saw or heard, and characterised by absolute certainty that what the prophet is proclaiming is not just his own thinking but the Word of God

The Three Major Elements of the Prophetic Books

— Oracles (e.g. Jeremiah 4-5)

— the usual form is poetic, easy to memorise, allowing the prophet to give the same message in various places, and his disciples to remember the oracle

— sometimes the oracles are given in prose form

— Biographical Material

— especially an account of the call of the prophet, which justifies the right of the prophet to speak in God's name (e.g. Amos 7:12-15)

— sometimes gives the context of a prophet's teaching or mission (e.g. Jeremiah 20:1-6)

— Continuation Material from the prophet's disciples (e.g. Isaiah 40-66)

— sometimes a prophet seems responsible for a whole school of theology which continues his thought in later years and changed circumstances; the material which results from this continuation is often included with the oracles of the original prophet (see Session Two on authorship)

Background to Jeremiah

— Jeremiah himself from a good family, of the priestly class

— a reluctant prophet who struggles with his vocation

— began his career during the reforming reign of Josiah, but the reformation did not last

— Judah had an uneasy pact with Assyria and Egypt, while the rival superpower, Babylon, was making its presence felt

— Jehoiakim, Josiah's son and (second) successor to the throne, was a pompous ruler, oblivious to the prophetic word and to the danger that the nation was in; once Babylon was established as the great power, Jehoiakim attempted an unsuccessful revolt

— Jeremiah found himself proclaiming a warning to a people and its rulers who did not give it serious consideration. Although this reaction caused him much personal suffering, he remained true to his calling and to the hope contained in his message

NOTES ON THE TEXT

1:4-8 Yahweh's call and Jeremiah's reluctant response. These verses contain incidental reference to the Old Testament belief that life and the divine plan for a person exist before birth. Jeremiah's answer is translated by Jerome's Vulgate as "A a a, Domine Deus" which reproduces the stuttering sound of the Hebrew.

1:9-10 The authority given the prophet is in part a destructive one, since there is much that must be changed in Judah; yet the note of hope is there too, in the building and planting.

1:11-12 An example of a prophecy that comes by internal inspiration. Jeremiah sees an almond tree (*shaqed* in Hebrew) which triggers the message that Yahweh is watching (*shoqed* in Hebrew) to ensure that his Word is done.

1:14-16 Another example of internal inspiration. The constant breaking of the covenant is about to bring down the curses of the covenant upon the nation.

4:1-4 The purpose of preaching destruction is not simple prediction of the vindictive action of a petty god: it is a call to repent, a last chance, which can change the course of history if acted upon.

4:10 In the day of disaster, Yahweh will be blamed for the false prophets who proclaimed peace in his name.

4:22 The two types of wisdom in the Letter of James are seen here, too, in the inhabitants of Jerusalem who are wise in evil and simpletons in doing good.

4:30; 5:7-8 The covenant with Yahweh was seen as a marriage between God and Israel, especially through the influence of a prophet like Hosea. It follows that those who are unfaithful to the covenant are considered adulterers, running after false gods like lovers. The analogy is helped by the fact that the pagan cults often involved temple prostitutes in their fertility rites.

5:1 The two extremes: Yahweh's extraordinary readiness to forgive is outweighed by the overwhelming and complete corruption of his people.

5:5 The Old Testament often lays the blame for the mistakes of the nation as a whole at the feet of the rulers, royal and priestly. If these do well with regard to Yahweh, then the whole people will follow.

5:13-14 Jeremiah has a high regard for the effectiveness of God's Word, even if people will not listen to it. The Word of God always has consequences implied to it: if you put the Word into practice, such and such will happen; if you ignore this Word, the opposite will happen. Instead of a blessing, the prophet's oracles bring a curse on those who dismiss it.

5:18 The message of destruction is not absolute; this verse and the following imply the prophetic hope of a remnant of the people surviving.

5:27-29 Yahweh is seen as the protector of social justice, especially of people who had no other protector (such as widows and orphans).

5:31 The priests and false prophets are giving the people what they want, but not what they need.

QUESTIONS FOR DISCUSSION

— What part does Jeremiah see God as playing in the current affairs of his time?

— What assurances does God give Jeremiah when he calls him to become a prophet? Does Jeremiah seem eager to say yes?

MATERIAL AND DISCUSSION QUESTIONS FOR SESSION SEVEN

Jeremiah 19-20, 30-31

— Is complaining to God an authentic way of praying?

— How does Christianity fulfill the promise of the New Covenant?

Another Look at Jeremiah
Jer 19-20, 30-31

In this age of the individual, some of the group are bound to notice that the community of God's people have been in the forefront of our foray into the Old Testament in contrast to much traditional Christian formation which often concentrated on individual salvation. Granted that community is a very important factor in scriptural thinking, the question can still arise: "Did the God of the Old Testament only care about people in bunches?" To balance out the perspective, Jeremiah 19-20 gives us a glimpse of an Old Testament relationship between Yahweh and an individual. In doing so, that passage can also teach us a new lesson on prayer.

The background is largely found in chapter 19. The prophet acts out a parable, smashing a jug to demonstrate the coming destruction of Jerusalem and the people of Judah. Then he goes back into the temple and preaches his message of disaster.

The temple would have been the scene of much teaching and preaching by all sorts of people, so there was nothing unusual in Jeremiah prophesying there. But the temple was no place for a message of coming destruction. In the popular mind, the Temple (as the place of God's dwelling among his people) was a sort of guarantee: as long as it stood, Jerusalem would stand, its political institutions would be secure, and everything would go well with Judah. But here was Jeremiah saying that this just wasn't true, that it was people obeying Yahweh that counted, not a building standing in the city. The seventh chapter of Jeremiah shows him proclaiming the same sort of message.

When one of the Temple officials, Pashhur the priest, heard Jeremiah's terrible message, he could not let the prophet go unpunished. He had him beaten and put into the public stocks, a sign of official disapproval and disavowal of Jeremiah's prophecy. This action was a religious punishment, and Jeremiah found himself out of favour with the religious establishment in charge of the official worship of Yahweh; to call it a type of Old Testament excommunication would not be too far wrong. But being put outside of the structures of Yahweh's people did not destroy Jeremiah's relationship with his Lord, and we can see the richness of this relationship in the prayer of chapter 20.

The prayer does not require a second reading to know that it is a prayer from the heart, and strong meat indeed. Still, the modern Christian can learn from Jeremiah that the authentic relationship with God spills out everything to him in prayer, not just the things that we feel God wants to hear. There is anger in his prayer, anger with the likes of Pashhur of course, but also anger with God. Being God's prophet has caused Jeremiah a lot of trouble (and it was to cause him more). Jeremiah wants to reject his vocation, but can't bring himself to do so. And so even this angry prayer has a note of confidence, that Yahweh will not ultimately see him abandoned. He feels let down, he is sorry that he was ever born, but he brings his complaint to the one who can do something about his predicament.

With all these messages of gloom, the reader should open Jeremiah 30-31 with the feeling of coming into a clearing in the forest. In fact, chapters 30 to 34 are often referred to as "The Book of Consolation". Many scholars feel that these chapters do not belong to the original oracles of Jeremiah, that they must be the work of later hands. But more recently there has been more of an openness to include at least part of these passages in Jeremiah's own material. In any case, the notion of hope was not alien to Jeremiah; the reason that he proclaimed coming disaster was in the hope that it would never happen, that Judah would turn to Yahweh and be saved. The Book of Consolation, whatever its origins, is now part of the theology of Jeremiah as it has entered the canon of inspired writings; to separate it from the rest would be to give only half the picture.

It can be noticed in chapter 30 that the message of comfort is linked to the message of destruction, the prediction of the Exile. The Exile will probably need explanation. Basically, it was the method of subduing and assimilating a conquered people by the conquering superpower. All of the potential leadership of the conquered nation was deported and a large "safe" population would be moved in to take over. Given a few generations of intermarriage, and the conquered nation no longer retained its identity. This is what happened to the so-called "Ten Lost Tribes of Israel": when the Northern Kingdom (Israel) fell in 721 BC, the Assyrians moved in a fresh population who intermingled with the native population still resident to produce the Samaritans. A Judaean view of the matter can be read in II Kings 17.

The ten lost tribes of Israel were not lost in the way you might think.

Exile was the fate facing the Southern Kingdom (Judah) in Jeremiah's time, and naturally the same prospect of being lost forever as a nation also faced them. But Jeremiah says no, Judah will remain as a nation and the land will be restored; but there will be a great spiritual improvement as a result. Chapter 31 insists on speaking as if the Northern Kingdom will also be restored, which implies that the restoration goes far beyond the punishment. Jeremiah's action of buying property in Judah in the face of calamity (Jer 32:1-15) like the words of hope show that the Exile would not last long enough for Judah's identity to be lost; the Exile ended with the Edict of Cyrus in 538 BC, less than fifty years after the destruction of Jerusalem.

MATERIAL

Jer 19-20, 30-31

AIM OF SESSION

To look at an example of personal relationship with the Lord in the Old Testament and to see the place of hope in the prophetic message.

SESSION NOTES (A)

An Old Testament Example of the Personal Relationship with God: Jer 19-20

— the Temple was a sign of security for the people of Jerusalem

— as long as the Temple stood, God was with his people, and no harm could come to them (see Jeremiah 7)

Jeremiah preached his message of doom in the Temple itself

— this violated the popular belief of Temple as security

— this was taken as a direct affront by the Temple authorities

Jeremiah was publicly punished for his prophecy

— rejected by the religious leadership of the covenant nation

— put outside the structures of the worship of Yahweh

— still maintained his relationship with the Lord, despite this rejection

Jeremiah's prayer, the prayer of a person in desperate circumstances

— complains to the one he feels is responsible

— complains to the one who can do something about the problem

— speaks what he feels, not what he thinks God wants to hear

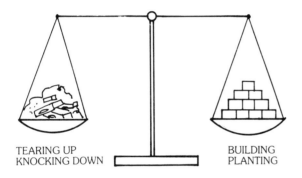

TEARING UP
KNOCKING DOWN

BUILDING
PLANTING

HOPE BALANCES JEREMIAH'S MESSAGE

NOTES ON THE TEXT (A)

19:1-11 The prophets, including the prophets at court and the bands of charismatic prophets, would often act out their message dramatically. This dramatised parable of the jug follows an image in chapter 18 where Yahweh is compared to a potter, working out the fate of the nations as a potter works out his designs on the clay.

19:14-15 Jeremiah prophesies destruction on the city from the Temple, an act that seemed blasphemous to those who prized the Jerusalem Temple as the sign of divine favour on the city.

20:1-6 The action of Pashhur is a public disclaimer of the message of Jeremiah. Pashhur's own punishment for resisting the Word of God will be to see that Word come true in his own family. Verse 6 indicates that Pashhur himself has acted the false prophet, giving God's people facile messages of consolation instead of encouraging them to repent.

20:7 The beginning of Jeremiah's prayer clearly shows that he feels unfairly treated by Yahweh, whose call has resulted in his misery.

20:9 Jeremiah attempts to resist the gift of prophecy, but he finds himself overwhelmed by it. The Old Testament sees the Word of God not just as an utterance but as a force of creation (as in Genesis 1) or for destruction (as in Jeremiah). The power of the Word is felt even in the man who acts as its vehicle, so that he cannot stop himself proclaiming it.

20:11-13 These verses show a spark of confidence in Yahweh's faithfulness. Often in a prayer of distress, the Old Testament concludes with a thanksgiving as if the cry for help has already been heard. The following verses show that this thanksgiving is not a sign that Jeremiah's despondency has lifted.

20:14 This section should be taken in the oratorical sense in which it was intended. A curse could be called on the day of Jeremiah's birth, since all the days that ever were were thought to be present to Yahweh at once: if he blotted it out, then it would never have happened.

SESSION NOTES (B)

The Book of Consolation

— chapters 30 to 34 sometimes called "The Book of Consolation" because of the hopeful tone it sets for Israel's future

— some scholars feel that much of it is written by those who continued Jeremiah's thought into later years (see Session Six); they find it hard to believe that Jeremiah himself could pronounce hope so strongly

— more recent thinking sees less problem about combining strong warning with hope:

  — the prophetic warning itself is a type of hope, hope that Israel will repent and that the predicted destruction will never come about

  — hope balances out the prophetic message; just as the prophet sees the sins of his people bringing down destruction, he also sees the faithful love of Yahweh as ensuring that something survives despite the destruction

— hope is as much a part of Jeremiah's message as the coming disaster; this can be seen in the word addressed to the prophet at the time of his call, not just tearing up and knocking down, but also building and planting. These words are echoed in the Book of Consolation (Jer 31:28)

— the hope takes the form of a reconstruction of Israel, a promise that the disintegration which faced the ten tribes of the north will not be realised for Judah during its Exile

— the restored Israel will be in a stronger relationship to its Lord, a new covenant of interior love (not just external observance) and of forgiveness

NOTES ON THE TEXT (B)

30:3 "The days are coming" is Jeremiah's way of speaking about the future hope throughout the Book of Consolation; the message does not annul the message of impending doom, but supplements it. Here the word of consolation presumes that the Exile will take place, but pronounces hope in the face of that inevitability.

30:10-11 A promise of homecoming for the exiles is linked with the statement that the now conquerers will some day no longer be a nation while Israel survives. Notice the use of the word "save" here has nothing to do with eternal destiny; in much of the Old Testament there was no awareness of an afterlife and "saving" was something to be done about present dangers, not eternal ones.

30:12-17 Only Yahweh who has caused such disaster for Israel can possibly effect the healing of the incurable wounds.

30:22-31:1 The chapter divisions are not part of the original text of the Bible, but added in the early Middle Ages for easy reference. Sometimes they can be confusing, seeming to separate material that belongs together, as in the case of these verses. The message is that Israel, now in the midst of confusing tragedy, will understand Yahweh's purpose of cleansing and renewal when the restoration comes.

31:2 The prophets often looked back to the wandering through the Sinai desert as a type of honeymoon between Yahweh and his people; the Exile will be a second honeymoon, a renewal of love.

31:5-6 "Samaria" and "Ephraim" imply a restoration of the long-fallen Northern Kingdom.

31:15-16 Rachel was the mother of the lost tribes of Ephraim and Manasseh; her sorrow will be comforted in the day of restoration. This verse is quoted in Mt 2:18.

31:21 The people going into exile are told to mark the road so that those making the return journey will know the way, a very strong promise that the exile will not last forever.

31:28 Echoes of Jer 1:10.

31:31-34 The promise of a New Covenant shows how thorough the remaking of the people will be, down to the roots of the Covenant itself. There might be a criticism of the reform of King Josiah here (see Session Six) — was it too concerned with the externals of religion and not enough with people's internal faith? The New Covenant is one of authenticity on the part of God's People and forgiveness on the part of Yahweh.

QUESTION FOR DISCUSSION

Is complaining to God an authentic way of praying?
How does Christianity fulfill the promise of the New Covenant?

MATERIAL AND DISCUSSION QUESTIONS FOR SESSION EIGHT

Psalms 29, 30, 88, 103, 105, 107

— Does anything in some of these psalms remind you of the prayer in Jeremiah 20?

— Does our picture of God tend to be more abstract than the picture of God in the psalms?

The Songs of Sion
Psalms 29, 30, 88, 103, 105, 107

No other Old Testament book has seen the scholarly advances or the popular treatment that the Book of Psalms has received in recent years. In the field of scholarship, much has been discovered (and debated) about the original cultic setting of the Psalms, the structure of their poetry, and even their language. The Psalms have also been a great area for popular exposition since patristic times (remember Augustine's homilies on the Psalms?), and their more prominent place in the revised liturgy gives that exposition added impetus in Catholic circles. An introductory talk cannot hope to explore all the riches, and not much of the scholarship; yet the group can discover some of the variety, vitality and spirituality of this collection of ancient hymns, even in one session.

The Psalms have been referred to as the whole Old Testament put into prayer; you can certainly find all the great themes and the more important ideas of the Old Testament somewhere in the one hundred and fifty psalms. The psalms use history and legend, the questions raised by Israel's wise men, the challenge of the prophets, and even the love of the Law. While some of the Old Testament was written as literature and some as law and some as record, the Psalms were written to be *used* in acts of worship, pieces of living liturgy. But their use in the solemn liturgies of the Temple was the first stage in a progression of uses which they were to receive. Especially during the exile, they became part of the smaller Liturgies of the Word of the synagogue. In the New Testament, the psalms take a pride of place among the Old Testament texts applied to Christ and the events which surround him. In the prayer of the Church, the psalms have taken on a new application (and a new level of meaning), being prayed constantly in the name of the whole Body of Christ: the laments are prayed in the name of the suffering members, the thanksgivings on behalf of the rejoicing members, and everything in the name of Christ the Head.

One of the greatest advances in the study of the psalms was in the early part of this century when they were broken into general categories by Hermann Gunkel. He was the scholar who insisted that in order to be fully understood, the psalms

Psalms were meant to be sung.

needed to be placed in their original setting in the Jerusalem Temple. He discerned six major categories among the psalms, and a handful of lesser ones. The first two categories, Individual Laments and Communal Laments, follow the same basic pattern. They begin with a cry to God, then give the reason for the call for help. This part of the psalm, the main body of the lament, might give a description of the petitioner's plight and all of his troubles; or it might say why it is to Yahweh that the prayer is addressed — maybe it is because the psalmist is so virtuous and faithful that God should rescue him, or maybe it is because the psalmist blames Yahweh for the mess he's in (see Psalm 88). Often the lament ends with a promise of praise or even an act of thanksgiving (see Psalm 31:21-24). This strange feature comes from the utter confidence that what help he needs will be forthcoming from God, so that the thanks can be made even before the help arrives.

Thanksgiving Psalms are the other end of the spectrum and form another of Gunkel's categories; they, too, can be either communal or individual. The thanksgiving has a circular form: it begins with a call to praise or an act of praise, goes on to

75

describe what Yahweh has done worthy of thanks, and ends where it begins with praise. Perhaps we should imagine that when the psalmist describes the problems from which he was released, that there was a dramatic enactment of his plight (try this with Psalm 118:5-14). The call to praise at the end gives the thanksgiving a prolonged quality: the note of praise echoes after the psalm itself has ended, taken up by those who have heard of Yahweh's mighty act.

Another group are psalms which celebrate God's Kingship, or Enthronement Psalms. Many scholars feel that there was an annual celebration of God's rule over Israel and the universe in the autumn (which later became the three feasts of the New Year, Day of Atonement, and Tabernacles), and that a major part of this celebration was a procession with the Ark of the Covenant ending with an enthronement in the holy of holies amidst cries of "Yahweh is King!" Any psalm which begins with that phrase belongs to this category, as does Psalm 29. This song celebrates Yahweh's presence in the storm and uses the image of Yahweh's mastery over the waters of sea and storm to speak of God's omnipotence. Psalm 29 also fits another of Gunkel's groupings, the Hymns of Praise, which praise Yahweh without reference to some mighty deed done for the psalmist. Another example of that category is to be found in Psalm 33 which describes Yahweh as worthy of confidence; the shortest psalm of all, Psalm 117, is also a hymn of praise which centres around the *ḥesed* and *'emeth* of Yahweh (Ps 117:2).

The final major category takes in the songs used for state occasions, the Royal Psalms. There are psalms which were obviously written for coronations and similar celebrations (Psalms 2, 72 and 110, for instance), and one psalm is for a royal wedding (Psalm 45). The Temple was next to the palace and somewhat dwarfed by it (Solomon needed the space for his seven hundred wives and three hundred concubines, and a whole section of the civil service probably to keep track of wedding anniversaries). Part of the reason for the Temple was to demonstrate in stone the strong relationship between God and the ruling dynasty (see session five), so it is only natural

that many of the ceremonies revolved around the King. This explains in part the close connection which later generations of readers saw between the Book of Psalms and David, the father of the Jerusalem dynasty: the obvious royal overtones of otherwise normal psalms (such as Psalm 18, an individual thanksgiving) could be accounted for by associating the psalms with the royal figure who also had a reputation for musical composition and liturgical arrangements (cf. 1 Sam 16:14-23 and 1 Chr 6:31; 16:4-7). Many of the psalms may have originally been composed for royal use, and afterwards become the common property of all worshippers of Yahweh; if so, our liturgical practice of praying them in the name of Christ the King has made them royal again.

There are many minor categories as well: psalms which tell of the history of Israel (such as Psalm 105), psalms which ponder the philosophical questions of the fate of the good and the evil (Psalm 1), psalms which deliver a prophetic punch (Psalm 50), and psalms which sing of the Law (Psalm 119). But all of these groupings are somewhat arbitrary: just because a psalm fits into one slot doesn't mean that it won't fit into one or two more. Identifying some of the types should help us to appreciate other psalms of the same type and to get a better feel for the spirituality of the psalms.

Hebrew poetry might also be introduced in this session. The primary point to get across is that Hebrew poetry rhymes ideas, not syllables, the phenomenon we call parallelism. This method is not familiar to the modern reader, and can be thought to be confusing at worst and boring at best; yet a few introductory words can make the whole matter clearer and help the reader to see the beauty of these ancient poems.

Basically, parallelism means that the idea of the first half-verse will be echoed in the second half-verse. Sometimes this can be done in the same terms:

> *Shout joyfully to God our strength*
> *Shout to the God of Jacob. (Ps 81:1)*

There is no real need for the second half-verse here, for the first half has said it all. But this repetitive style is the very heart of

Hebrew poetry. It can do other tricks, however, like give the other half of the thought:

> With Yahweh shepherding me
> I have no need. (Ps 23:1)

Or maybe the same thought can be expressed through its opposite:

> Give ear, God, to my prayer
> and do not hide from my petition. (Ps 55:1)

Or the second half-verse can fill in a metaphor in the first:

> As far away as east from west
> he has put far away from us our sins. (Ps 103:12)

Parallelism is worth exploring, for it is a whole way of thinking. Even the words of Jesus in the gospels show evidence of parallel thought:

> The things which are Caesar's give over to Caesar
> And the things which are God's to God. (Mk 12:17)

> I am the Way and the Truth and Life
> No one comes to the Father except through me. (Jn 14:6)

The Psalter is the prayer book of the Bible, and many of the other prayers scattered around the Old and New Testaments take their pattern from the psalms. After this session, there should be a conscious effort to utilise the psalms more and more into the group's prayer together and so to place them into their natural habitat.

MATERIAL
Psalms 29, 30, 88, 103, 105, 107

AIM OF SESSION
To introduce the psalms in the context of their types and forms and Temple setting; to show simply the mechanics of parallelism in Hebrew poetry.

SESSION NOTES

Introducing the Book of Psalms
— No other Old Testament book so extensively used by the Christian Church

— No other Old Testament book has been the subject of such scholarly advances

— The Psalter contains the building blocks of the whole Old Testament (legend, history, wisdom, prophecy, law) and puts them into prayer

— History gave to the psalms different uses, applications, and levels of meaning:
  — the original Temple usage for which most of them were composed

  — during and after the exile, formed the basis of synagogue spirituality

  — instead of being limited to important Temple ceremonies, the Psalms become the prayers of every person in every situation

  — the Book of Psalms (to judge by New Testament evidence) was the prayer book of the early Christians, including Jesus himself.

— in the New Testament, the psalms are especially applied to Christ and his work and the events of his life (e.g. Mk 12:36; Lk 20:17; Jn 13:18; Acts 1:20; Eph 4:8; Heb 1:5, 8-13)

  — prayed by the Church today
  — as individual members
  — in the name of the whole Body of Christ (in the Office)

77

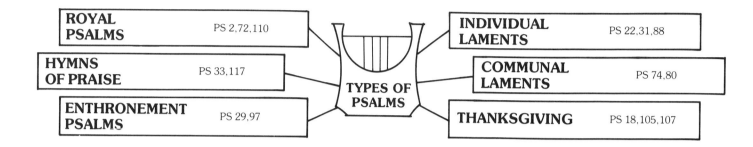

The Original Setting of the Psalms:
— started as songs for use in the Temple liturgies
— the Temple was the only place of official worship in all of Israel; part of the palace complex in Jerusalem

— many think that the psalms should be thought of as closely connected with royal and state ceremonies

— certainly the Temple setting would have meant instrumental music, choirs and soloists, and liturgical dancing (see Ps 150)

— not composed to be read or listened to as much as to be *used*: the Book of Psalms is not an anthology of literary poetry, but fragments of a living liturgy.

— remembering the cultic setting of the psalms, it can be useful to divide them into groups which share similar structure or theme; Gunkel pointed out these six major groups, and many smaller ones:
— Individual Laments (where one person, often the king, is in trouble)

— Communal Laments (where the whole nation is in trouble)

— Individual and Communal Thanksgivings (when the trouble is over)

— Enthronement Psalms (for celebrating Yahweh's Kingship)

— Hymns of Praise (for praise of Yahweh for his mighty deeds)

— Royal Psalms (for use at the king's wedding or coronation)

The Psalms as Poetry: Types of Parallelism
— repeating the same idea in different words (Ps 81:1)

— or repeating the idea through its opposite (Ps 35:1)

— or filling in a metaphor (Ps 103:12)

— or giving the other half of the thought (Ps 23:1)

NOTES ON THE TEXT

Ps 29 This psalm belongs to two of the major groupings, primarily being a Hymn of Praise, it also celebrates Yahweh's kingship and could be called an Enthronement Psalm. Yahweh makes his presence felt in the storm, the thunder being his voice, and all of creation trembles at the theophany. This also expresses Yahweh's kingship over all, which means that Israel will be blessed for being the people of the Universal King.

Ps 30 An Individual Thanksgiving which loosely fits the general pattern: an act of praise, description of Yahweh's deed which merits the thanksgiving, and an act of praise at the end. The initial act of praise in verse one is elaborated in verses four and five, the vivid description of the trouble and deliverance is in verses six to eleven, and the concluding act of praise is in verse twelve. This pattern also holds good for Communal Thanksgivings.

Ps 88 Individual Laments usually begin with an invocation, proceed to give the reasons why the call for help is made (perhaps a description of the problem, perhaps a plea of innocence), and conclude with a promise or act of thanksgiving. This psalm conforms to the pattern with the exception of the praise, and the reason is no mystery: the psalmist blames Yahweh for all the problems. It is *his* anger that crushes, Yahweh has removed health and friends. Notice the attitude towards life after death in verses ten to twelve: the psalmist tells Yahweh to help him while he can still return thanks and service.

Ps 103 One of the most beautiful of the Hymns of Praise, this psalm also gives fine examples of parallelism and metaphor in verses eleven to thirteen. One way of approaching this psalm would be to consider it an extended meditation on Yahweh's *ḥesed* (a word which occurs four times in the psalm).

Ps 105 Believe it or not, this psalm is a Communal Thanksgiving, or at least it is a meditation on Israel's history framed as a thanksgiving. History for the biblical person was never something over and done with; it made the present and involved all those living in the present, and that was especially true of central events, such as the Exodus. Here the Exodus is viewed as the working out of the covenant promise to Abraham (verses seven to eleven and forty-two), and the psalm begins and ends with the act of the praise characteristic of the thanksgiving (verses one to four and forty-five). The historical thanksgiving form is not unlike the fourth Eucharistic Prayer of the Roman missal.

Ps 107 This unique thanksgiving seems to have been meant for a group celebration, perhaps even with the different worshippers arranged according to the reason for their thanksgiving. Each section follows the same pattern: first a description of the plight of the desert wanderer, or the seafarer, or whatever, then how they invoked God's help with a description of how Yahweh responded to their need. The whole thanksgiving ends with a summary of God's wonderful deed (verses thirty-three to thirty-eight) and of his constant love for his people (verses thirty-nine to forty-three).

QUESTIONS FOR DISCUSSION

— Does anything in some of these psalms remind you of the prayer in Jeremiah 20?

— Does our picture of God tend to be more abstract than the picture of God in the psalms?

MATERIAL AND DISCUSSION QUESTIONS FOR SESSION NINE

St Paul's Letter to the Galatians
— Is there a contradiction between Paul and James?

— Is justification by faith stressed enough in our Church?

Paul and Faith
The Letter to Galatians

Just to mention St Paul in certain circles might be dangerous. Don't like him — too stern; the man needed cheering up." "Didn't he hate women or something?" The exposure which Paul has had in recent years through the new Lectionary and such may have improved his standing with some people, but in general, Paul could have done with a better press agent. This role now is inherited by the Bible Group leader, whose approach should be to demonstrate the heart of Paul's thinking rather than get side-tracked into his less popular traits.

Since Paul tended to write in letters to specific communities, letters occasioned by real needs and problems, this is the place to introduce the notion of *sitz im leben,* or *living situation* (for those who don't like German). This means that the understanding of a piece of writing is greatly improved once we understand: a) the use for which it was intended and b) the audience to which it was addressed. This is a notion which the session notes have been using all along: we have already looked at the audience when studying the Letter of James, and in dealing with the Psalms, we investigated their original use and setting. Ignorance of the living situation can lead to grave error in getting at the message of a piece of writing: imagine reading a form letter with the same intensity as a personal letter, or an advertisement in a newspaper as if it were the result of investigative reporting! One of the major advances in biblical scholarship of this century has been the recognition of the importance of setting the Scriptures firmly against the background of their living situations (an advance made by the school known as the form critics).

So the first question to be asked about the Letter of the Galatians is "Who are the Galatians?" The term normally applies to a people who inhabited the interior region of Asia Minor. These people were Celtic, far removed cultural and racial cousins of the ancient Gauls (note the similarity of name). For this reason, the letter has been jokingly referred to as "St Paul's Letter to the Irish" — which isn't too complimentary to the Irish if you read the letter. Galatia was also a regional term as well as an ethnic one, and it covers the missions of Paul recorded in Acts 13:13-14:27 (as well as those in Acts 16:1-6).

First question. "who are the Galatians?"

If this be the case, then the letter is not addressed to Celtic Galatians, but to people of other ethnic backgrounds living in the southern regions of the administrative province of Galatia.

Whichever group they were, they were evangelised by Paul himself, only to alter that gospel message because of later preachers. We call Paul the Apostle of the Gentiles, which means that his mission was to those of pagan stock. For him, there was one basic requirement for the Gentiles to enter the people of God: faith in Christ and his message, and a life that corresponded to that faith.

Close on Paul's heels came other preachers. They thought that there was something else necessary to become a Christian. Their line of reasoning may have been something like this: to have part in Christ is to share in all the blessings of the covenant with Abraham, for Christ is the fulfilment of the promises made to Abraham. Now God told Abraham to have himself circumcised. Therefore, if anyone is to attach himself to God's people in Christ, circumcision should be a requirement. On top of this, other bits and pieces of the Mosaic Law should be observed by the former pagan.

Paul isolates the conflict as a matter of *justification,* that is, what is it that makes a person right with God? Paul, it should be remembered, was a Pharisee before his conversion, someone who studied the Mosaic Law in the greatest detail to discover how to avoid breaking it. The Pharisee stands up to brag to God about how much he's doing to increase his heavenly bank balance. The Pharisee's approach is to be right with God by keeping the Law and doing acts of piety. It sounds good on paper, but Paul's greatest objection is that, in fact, no one *does* keep the Law; if we are put right with God, it is because of his gracious forgiveness and love rather than any great thing that we do for him. This is the heart of what Paul means by justification by faith, as explained in Romans 1-8. The Law is useless to bring us to salvation; it shows its uselessness by pronouncing a curse on Christ (Gal 3:13), and when it does that, you know that the Law is no longer a reliable guide. So, for the Christian, faith has replaced Law to put people right with God.

But what does Paul mean by faith? To us, faith is an intellectual affair, a matter of belief. This, to some extent is what James meant by faith. For Paul, and most of Scripture, faith is far more active. The Greek word for faith, *pistis*, is closely related to the word faithful, *pistos*, and does itself have the connotation of remaining steadfast, being faithful. The Greek translation of the Old Testament sometimes uses *pistis* to translate our old friend *'emeth*, covenant faithfulness, to which the Hebrew word for faith is closely related.

Paul concedes to his opponents, the "Judaisers", that to join God's people means to become part of Abraham's family. The Judaisers say that this is done by circumcision of the males, since that is what happened in Abraham's day and ever since among the Jews. Paul agrees that this is what happened, but says that something else justified Abraham. In Galatians 3:6, Paul refers to something that happened before circumcision ever appeared on the scene, when Scripture says that Abraham was justified when he put his faith in Yahweh (Gen 15:6). This, Paul holds, and not circumcision is what brings us into Abraham's clan and makes people inheritors of all the promises. Actually for Paul there is only one heir, Christ himself; we become part of him through faith and share in the inheritance (Gal 3:15-16; see Session Five on Corporate Personality).

This should help explain why Abraham has such prominent mention here and elsewhere in the New Testament: in order to benefit from Christ, one must become a member of Abraham's family. In New Testament times, the Jews would admit pagans to their ranks through circumcision, and the converts were deemed to be heirs of Abraham. Paul says that circumcision only admits you to Abraham's family on a physical level; faith in Christ does the trick for the spiritual reality. Paul utilises the fact that Abraham had a son who did not become heir to the covenant, Ishmael, born from the slave-girl Hagar. Paul tells us that this was because Ishmael was not born because of the spiritual promise of a son, but simply because of the physical relationship between Hagar and Abraham; the child of the promise was Isaac, born of the aged Sarah because of the promise which God had made. Paul makes an allegory to say that those who are circumcised and follow the Law might be in a physical relationship to Abraham, but they won't necessarily be in line to inherit the promises; the real descendants and heirs are the ones who take after Abraham in a spiritual way, by following his faith, and these are the ones who will see all the promises come true for them.

We can sympathise with the "foolish Galatians" who were so quick to strive after religious accomplishments and rules and regulations. Man always wants spiritual bargaining power, to be able to stand up and say to God, "Look at everything I'm doing for you", as if the love of God must be earned. To depend on faith seems to make us so vulnerable; and yet to Paul, no less than to James, faith makes as much demand on our lives as Law and more demands on our hearts. But justification by faith is a reminder that when we are before God we are in a position of begging rather than bragging, and that our begging brings us the riches of forgiveness and favour and love.

MATERIAL

Paul's Letter to the Galatians

AIM OF SESSION

To situate the Letter to the Galatians in the conflict between Paul and the Judaisers; to show Paul's thought on justification by faith.

SESSION NOTES

The Living Situation (*Sitz Im Leben*):

— The proper interpretation of any piece of writing depends on some awareness of its setting.

— we do this automatically with material encountered in our own culture, such as advertisements, form letters, etc.

At a minimum, we should try to assess the living situation of a text in Scripture in two areas:

— the use for which it was originally intended and the reason for which it was written;

— the audience to which it was addressed

Paul's letters were originally written as letters to specific people because of specific problems and needs (with the exception of the Letter to the Romans).

— the Galatians were inhabitants of the province of Galatia, either the Celtic people who lived in the interior of Asia Minor or those (non-Celts) along the southern regions of Asia Minor whom Paul evangelised in an early mission (Acts 13:13-14:27)

— Paul's preaching was faith in Jesus Christ; certain opponents followed him to tell Paul's converts that they were also bound by Old Testament legalities, notably circumcision

— these "Judaisers" held that in order to benefit from the Messiah promised to the Jews, you had to be a member of Abraham's family, and that you were brought into that family by circumcision

— Paul isolated the problem as one of *justification*, or how a person is put right with God

Justification

— the Pharisees felt that man was justified by rigidly keeping the commandments of the Old Testament Law and doing good works

— Jesus criticises this position in Lk 18:9f

— Paul, having been trained as a Pharisee, would have held this position before his conversion.

— Paul rejects any idea that we can be justified by the good we do and by our own innocence.

— no one really keeps the Law anyway (Gal 3:10-12)

— the Law even pronounces a curse on Jesus (Gal 3:13)

— therefore the Law cannot make us right with God, only show how far we are from him (Gal 3:21-22)

— Paul points to faith as the way in which we are justified

Faith

— Paul's concept of faith is much richer and deeper than the usual meaning which we give to the term

— our notion of faith is often the same as belief, a purely intellectual activity; this is the notion which the Letter of James holds up as useless if not translated into action

— the Greek word (*pistis*) also has connotations of trust and of being faithful; it is sometimes used to translate the Hebrew word *'emeth*, covenant faithfulness

— Paul's idea of faith must be thought of as a full commitment of the whole person in trust to God through Christ

If anything brings the former pagan into Abraham's family, it is to imitate Abraham's faith.

— Abraham himself was justified through faith (Gal 3:6-9; Gen 15:6)

— Abraham was not a man of the Law, since the Law came with Moses a few hundred years later (Gal 3:17-18)

— Christ (the corporate Christ, all who form one Body with him) is the real heir to the promises of Abraham (Gal 3:15-16; 4:21ff)

There is a fundamental difference between justification by faith and attempting to justify ourselves by keeping the Law.

— dependence on our own keeping of the Law undermines the trusting faith attitude (Gal 5:1-6)

— the Law by nature is negative, whereas faith and the spirit are positive, spurring us on to higher things (Gal 5:16-23)

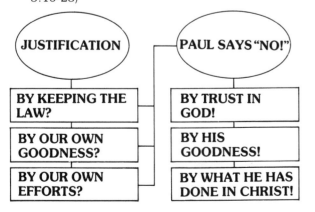

1:1-5 Paul in writing to his communities follows the general patterns of letters, starting with an address and form of greeting.

1:6-13 The gospel of the Judaisers is judged to be a radical departure from Paul's message, and Paul reserves some of the strongest wording in Scripture for these distorters, both here and later in the epistle.

1:14-20 Paul defends his credentials and the credentials of the gospel which he has preached, that he received a revelation of Christ upon which his preaching is based. Although he was not dependant on those who were apostles before him, he received their approval in his mission. Much ink has been spilt over the question of whether Gal 2:1-10 refers to the Council of Jerusalem or not, which it probably does.

2:15-21 Paul's own experience shows that the Law cannot make us blameless before God; Christ's whole mission, and especially his death, was to bring the salvation that the Law could never bring.

3:6-9 Abraham is introduced as the example of one justified by faith without the Law.

3:10-18 The various deficiencies of the Law are indicated: no one can keep it in entirety; it depends on external observance rather than interior faith; it places a curse on Christ; it only enters the scene hundreds of years after the promise of salvation to Abraham.

3:19-29 The Law may have had its uses, but it was only a temporary measure until the coming of faith in Christ. It should be noted that verse twenty-eight does not deny these distinctions make any difference in secular matters, or even in matters of Church order, but that despite these distinctions, all share equally in the salvation of faith.

4:3-5 Christ's coming brings in the full height of God's plan.

4:6-8 The calling which the Galatians had received was made known on a much more spiritual plane than keeping the Law, not the subservience of slaves, but the freedom of adopted children.

4:17-20 Paul casts aspersions on the motives of the Judaisers; they seem more concerned with extending their own influence than in the genuine good of the Galatians.

4:21-31 Physical descent from Abraham counts for nothing. If one is to be heir to the promise given Abraham, then one must be his descendant according to the terms of the promise, which is the freedom of faith.

5:13-21 Freedom is not licentiousness. We are freed from the concerns of legalism so that we can live by the dictates of the spirit. Those who use freedom for licentiousness will be excluded from the kingdom.

5:22-23 The fruit of the spirit which should be ripening in the life of the Christian is completely different to the life of carnal desires.

6:1-10 The freedom of the spirit brings personal responsibility for one's conduct together with some responsibility for mutual correction. Paul, it will be noted, is far from being against "good works", just against making these the basis of our hope. Our hope is not in our own efforts, but in what God has done and is doing for us.

6:14-16 A final statement that it is not circumcision but Christ's cross that makes the difference. The Galatians of pagan stock are full members of God's People and Abraham's family, and so are members of the "Israel of God".

QUESTIONS FOR DISCUSSION

— Is there a contradiction between Paul and James?

— Is justification by faith stressed enough in our Church?

MATERIAL AND DISCUSSION QUESTIONS FOR SESSION TEN

The Gospel of John, Chapter One
— What do we mean by calling Christ "the Word"?

— How does Jn 1:1-18 summarise the whole gospel message?

Tenth Session
Meeting John's Gospel

John 1:1-18

The study of a gospel with beginners has both advantages and disadvantages. Since most people have had some exposure to the gospel material since tender age, they have formed certain ideas about it which are hazardous: their presumptions about the gospels can lead them away from an enriching appreciation of the text.

A common idea of a gospel is that it is more or less a biography of Jesus; this is a notion which scholars have been trying to bludgeon for years, but it still has a lot of life in it yet. Certainly a gospel has a great deal of biographical material available on Jesus. But one of the reasons for not calling a gospel simple "biography" is that the gospel and a biography have different functions. Usually a biography is about someone remote, either too famous or too dead for the reader to have much contact with; the primary emphasis in biography is on things past. The gospel is about things present, about a living person with whom the reader will hopefully have much contact, a living relationship. The stories contained in the gospel may be past events, but they are stories about the same sort of thing which Jesus is doing today and which he can do in the lives of the readers. That is the big difference between the life of Jesus as painted in the gospel and a biography of Napoleon.

Rather than a biography, we should think of a gospel as a study, a word portrait of someone whom we have either met or that we are going to meet. Studying the gospel should have all the excitement of getting to know someone, either for the first time or as a deepening of a relationship. Biographies often conclude with the death of their subject; the gospels conclude with the Resurrection, with the statement that Jesus is still doing the type of activity which characterised his earthly life. For this reason, a gospel is a document of faith. It makes no pretence to objectivity, to telling the facts in a cool, critical, non-involved manner. John's Gospel exposes his hand in Jn 20:31 when he says, "These things are written so that you might believe that Jesus is the Messiah, the Son of God, and so that, being people of faith, you might have life in his name." There's not much disinterested journalism there! This thrust of faith moves in two directions: when read by believers, the gospel should strengthen the relationship between the Christian and Jesus; when read by the non-believer, the gospel tries to present an opportunity for faith by showing the person the demands of Jesus clearly. This can also mean that at times the material is presented in such a way as to help the reader over potential stumbling blocks (an apologetic approach); such stumbling blocks might be "How can a Jewish Messiah be rejected by his own people?" or "How could the Son of God be subject to such a shameful death?"

Another notion which many people have about the gospels is that they are basically simple documents written by unlettered fishermen. Certainly we can say that the gospels are not "scientific biographies", that is, using material which is well researched, compared with different sources, critically evaluated, and so on. In that aspect, the gospels are a bit naive: it would have not worried the evangelists that there are huge differences in the story of the blind man/men of Jericho (compare Mk 10:46 with Mt 20:29-30 and Lk 18:35) since the story of what Jesus does for those who turn to him remains identical in all three tellings, despite the discrepancies of detail.

But the gospels are "scientific" works, that is, well thought out and planned, using the stories and sayings to bring out a clear picture of what the author intends. We could re-state that by saying that most differences between the four gospels can be accounted for by the fact that each gospel presents its own theology. It does this by emphasising certain themes, by repeating scenes and by arranging material in a given order. In Mark's Gospel, for example, the whole story builds up to Peter's confession of faith in Mk 8:29 and from that point all emphasis is placed on the cross in Jerusalem. Mark makes the cross more clearly seen as the necessary consequence of Jesus being the Messiah by the way he arranges material in the gospel.

Each gospel has its own theology, but the picture of Jesus which most Christians have is a collage from the four gospels together (with bits and pieces from other places, too). Studying a gospel fully, then, will require a bit of discipline in sticking to

The Gospel is a word portrait of Christ, not a photograph.

85

the gospel in question if that evangelist's special theology is to be appreciated. If in discussion of one gospel members of the group drag in another gospel, there should be a reminder that this material is somewhat alien to the picture of the gospel being studied; we could never appreciate the Sistine Chapel if someone insisted on pasting prints of the Mona Lisa over it. The four gospels give us four theologies; we are the losers if we pretend that there is only one theology and not four.

Over the remaining sessions, we will take a careful look at the theology contained in John's Gospel. Other questions about the gospel will arise in the process and will be handled as we come across them. The first question, of course, is the origin of the gospel, and there are quite a few theories to choose from. It should be noted that the whole style and approach of John's Gospel differs from the first three gospels which share some of their sources and therefore much of their material. John's Gospel is unique in its material and in its outlook, which means that it had a different source. Our working hypothesis of its origins might be stated in this way: the Gospel of John reflects a Galilean background and its claim to be the testimony of an eyewitness (Jn 19:35; 21:24) can be taken to be authentic. There are definite signs that the work has been edited, but the sources are relatively uniform. The tradition which connects the Fourth Gospel with the apostle John is not contradicted by any of this, and so we can use the name for both the author of this work and the apostle; yet we mustn't imagine that John ever saw the gospel in its present state. He wasn't an author in the modern sense of the term, but the figure upon whose testimony and theological insight the whole work rests. If questions of authorship intrigue you, then the introduction to any full-scale commentary on the Fourth Gospel will give you plenty to think about.

John's theology has two questions at the hub: "Who is Christ?" and "What is the work of Christ?" He is notorious for being the most blatantly theological of the evangelists, which has earned him the title "John, the Divine" (from the old meaning of "divine" as "theologian") and the symbol of the eagle (soaring in the highest realms of theological thought).

John also communicates with gentle ambiguities, showing how people take Jesus up in the wrong way or are mistaken about his meaning. He uses puns which are lost in translation (we will point some of these out as they occur) and portrays Jesus as someone who enjoys teasing a person towards the truth. If you like the "Sermon on the Mount" type of teaching found in the first three gospels, you would be wasting your time trying to find it in John. All of his teaching is centred in the person and work of Christ, and in the relationship of the reader to the Father and to Jesus; even the miracles of this gospel seem to be pointers to this relationship.

A first-time reader of John's Gospel might find him a bit repetitive: first he says a thing one way, then says it again from a different angle and might say it a third or fourth time if the mood takes him. The last half of chapter six, for instance, repeats explicitly that Jesus is the living bread four times, and comes near enough to it in slightly different words a half dozen more. Modern logic demands that we speak in lines of thought (make the first point, leave it and make the second, leave it and make the third point, and so on) whereas John speaks in concentric ways (make a point, broaden it, broaden it again, and so on). With a bit of patience we can get into John's way of thinking and see that he is not quite as repetitive as we first suspected.

One technique John uses is debate and misunderstanding. Perhaps it is because John himself, like the other apostles, misunderstood Christ so much until the cross and resurrection, that he can use the misunderstanding. There is more than a bit of the poet in John, so we wouldn't be surprised to find that his symbols and wordings are often very rich with overtones.

The only text to be covered in this session is the Prologue of the gospel which doesn't even constitute a full chapter of the gospel. That can be misleading, since the Prologue can be seen as containing something of the whole message of the Fourth Gospel. It uses terms like "Word" and "Life" and "Light" to speak of the meaning of Christ in summary form, to say that Christ is the message of the Father in flesh and blood, that he is the Eternal Life given to those who believe, that he is the only real light shining in a dark world. John may have taken an early hymn about Christ and inserted into it statements about the Baptist so that the whole Prologue forms an arch, each side reflecting the other, with the keystone statement in verse 12. This technique, called *chiasm*, demonstrates just how carefully the gospels are constructed for their theological goals. John the son of Zebedee may have been a good fisherman, but he was a much better theologian.

MATERIAL

John 1:1-18

AIM OF SESSION

To make the distinction between gospel and biography; to identify the main thrusts of John's Gospel; to examine the prologue of the gospel.

SESSION NOTES

What is the Gospel?

— the word itself means Good News (in Greek, *euangelion*); it is the good news that the messiah has come in Jesus.

— the common idea that the four gospels are biographies of Christ could be very misleading:

— the gospels use biographical material, but they have a higher purpose than just telling us the facts about Jesus

— a biography could be said to talk mainly about the past; the gospels are speaking about the type of action Jesus did and words Jesus spoke in the past, *but that he is also doing and saying in the present*

— the gospels should be thought of, not as biographies, but as studies or portraits of someone that we can meet today; the reading of the gospel itself should present us with an opportunity to meet Christ and to form a living relationship with him.

— the gospels are documents of *faith*, not disinterested journalism

— they speak for the deep faith of the authors and sources

— they speak for the sake of the faith of the reader (Jn 20:30-31)

— to instill faith in the non-believer
— to deepen and renew faith in the believer

— the way that the gospels are written will be influenced by their concern over faith, to answer the questions of potential believers or to show the implications of a story for those who follow Jesus

The Gospels are primarily Theological Works

— we have four gospels because each of the four contains a unique theology, a unique picture of Christ and his work

— the differences between the gospels can best be seen as differences in their theologies

— the gospels use themes and arrangements to bring out their individual theologies (such as Mark's placing of Peter's confession at the half-way point of the gospel)

— for this reason, the full effect of a gospel can only be felt by reading a gospel from cover to cover, not by bits here and there

— the gospels were never meant to be scientific, critical biographies, but they were meant to be well-thought out works of theology

87

John's Gospel – an Introduction

— John's Gospel is quite different in tone and material to the first three gospels (which are often called the "synoptics")

— there have been many varied theories about its origins over the years; from our present knowledge we can be fairly sure that:

    — the gospel reflects a Palestinian and probably Galilean back-ground

    — there are no solid grounds to contest that the gospel rests on eyewitness testimony (Jn 19:35; 21:24)

    — the present work is a later edition of earlier material which seems to have come from a unified source

— the earlier source behind the present gospel is identified by tradition as the apostle John

John's theology centres around two basic questions

— Who is Christ?
— What is the work of Christ?

— not a lot of "Sermon on the Mount" type teaching in John's Gospel

— John is the most theological of the evangelists (called "John the Divine" and pictured as the eagle soaring lofty heights)

— the whole gospel is centred on the relationship of the reader to Christ and the Father (thus the most "sacramental" of the gospels)

John has his own style in presenting his message

— his argument is concentric and not linear

— instead of making the point and moving on to the next one, John makes a point and enlarges it and enlarges it again

— John is fond of plays on words and ambiguities

— he uses debates between different parties in a story and the misunderstanding of by-standers to bring home his message

— the sense of humour of Jesus comes across best in John's Gospel when he playfully confuses those whom he is drawing to himself

— because John is so theological, his stories and discourses are often rich in symbolism and overtones.

NOTES ON THE TEXT

1:1-18 This passage, usually called the prologue of the gospel, may have been a hymn which is reworked to serve as an introduction to the whole Fourth Gospel. The verses form a type of arch building up to and leading down from the high point in verse 12. The diagram shows how this works.

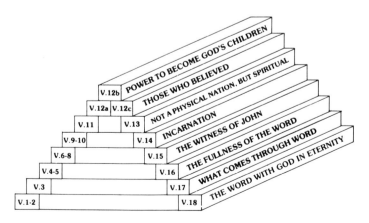

1:1 The Word (Greek: *Logos*) is a very rich term; its Hebrew equivalent means both word and action. Perhaps the best way to approach it is to think of Jesus as the whole message of God. This verse also contains an explicit statement of Christ's divinity which is re-echoed in Jn 20:28.

1:4 Light has lost its archetypal impact in our age of electricity, but John uses it as an image for the contrast between Christ and every other way of thinking and living. This "black and white" mentality is a Semitic way of thinking which is very much in evidence in the Fourth Gospel.

1:10 "The World" (Greek: *cosmos*) has a double aspect in John's Gospel: on the one hand, it is the world of mankind which God loves and tries to bring to himself (cf. Jn 3:17); but on the other hand, it can refer to the world which mankind has made, a world which reacts to Jesus with hatred and rejection, and it is usually this second meaning which we find in John's Gospel. *Cosmos* denotes order, the opposite of *chaos; it is akin to "system".*

1:11-13 The Word comes to his own people, but when he is rejected by them he is accepted by others. Those who were his people were such by virtue of physical descent, but now men and women are born into God's people by God rather than by natural longings and marital relations.

1:14 The Word doesn't just plunge himself into humanity, but becomes part of it, throwing up his tent alongside ours. The terms "grace and truth" as seen by some scholars as being translations of the covenant terms *ḥesed* and *'emeth*, that the real covenant relationship comes with Christ (see verse 17).

1:18 The original reading of this verse seems to have been "The Only-Begotten God" has made the Father known, but some later manuscripts changed this to "The Only-Begotten Son", and many translations follow the later form.

QUESTIONS FOR DISCUSSION

What do we mean by calling Christ "the Word"?
How does John 1:1-18 summarise the whole gospel message?

MATERIAL AND DISCUSSION QUESTIONS FOR SESSION ELEVEN

John 1:19-3:36

— How important is John the Baptist in this first part of the Fourth Gospel?

— Did Christ come for judgement or not?

Light Begins to Dawn
John 1:19-3:36

Perhaps the arrangement of this section of the Gospel might seem a little haphazard at first, but there are threads which can be traced in its fabric. One is the figure of John the Baptist, who is prominent here and then is to be found nowhere else in the gospel. Then there are ideas such as newness and descent from a higher realm, and two passages when it is hard to tell whether it is the evangelist speaking or one of the characters in the scene he has just described.

First, to consider the Baptist. It was a burning question in the days when the gospel was written as to the importance of John the Baptist, especially in relation to Jesus. There were people who could be described as disciples of the Baptist who were not disciples of Christ (cf. Acts 19:1-5), and part of the material dealing with John the Baptist undoubtedly deals with this question. If we accept that the source for the gospel lies in the unnamed disciple of Jesus (sometimes called "the Beloved Disciple"), then the author himself says that he was once one of John's followers (cf. Jn 1:35-40). His whole portrayal of John is meant to be of John's witness to Jesus; to place John the Baptist above Christ is to go against the whole thrust of what John was trying to do. John's diminishing role is moved towards its vanishing point by a careful intertwining of episodes concerning John with episodes showing the increasing activity and influence of Jesus. The pattern of this intertwining has already been set in the Prologue.

The notion of "newness" rings loudly three times in this section. The first toll is at the wedding of Cana, the second is in the cleansing of the Temple and the third is during the discussion with Nicodemus. All three of these introduce themes which will be developed as the gospel unfolds, typical of John's concentric method of reasoning (see Session Ten).

The wedding feast of Cana speaks of a newness of creation: water, which sometimes stands in the Bible for all of God's blessings (such as in Ezek 47 or Rev 22) is transformed into something richer and better in nearly unlimited quantity (six stone water jars at up to twenty-seven gallons a jar makes a total in the region of 972 modern bottles of wine!) We catch a glimpse here of the way that John treats physical reality,

Six stone jars equals 972 modern bottles of wine.

pointing out the way that it can tell us something beyond itself: water here becomes wine, bread becomes a sign of living bread, water elsewhere points to the living water, and so on. Some would even see in this miracle a eucharistic overtone: as water becomes something more precious in wine, so wine becomes more precious in the Eucharist.

The cleansing of the Temple takes on an added importance for John, as we can tell by his placing it at the start of the ministry, rather than at the end. This new location means that the incident is going to speak of the whole activity of Jesus. But before we consider that, we must rid ourselves of the image of temple as a sort of large parish church. The Temple was much more: it was the only place on earth where the Jews believed that God lived among his people; it was the one and only place where sacrifice could be offered to Yahweh; and it was to the Temple that the Jews were to come in pilgrimage at the great feasts of the year. When Christ describes himself as the Temple, he is saying that he alone is the new meeting place between God and man. So here we have a newness of worship, a new relationship between people and God, not localised in a place on earth, but in the person of Jesus himself.

The third note of newness depends on a pun in Greek; Jesus speaks of the need to be born *anōthen*, which Nicodemus takes to mean simply "again" while Christ puts the emphasis on its other meaning, "from above". The playfulness of Christ can also be seen in another pun in this incident, when he begins speaking about the wind (*pneuma* in Greek) and ends up talking about the Spirit (also *pneuma* in Greek). This birth, which is both new and from above, is entry into the new life, eternal life, which is at the heart of John's Gospel. (Incidently, the fact that the *anōthen* pun works only in Greek is one shred of evidence that Jesus may have spoken that language often, as well as Aramaic.)

"From above" is itself a main theme in the gospel, and in the section under study. Certainly the prologue describes the incarnation from the viewpoint of Christ's heavenly origins, and there are several connections made between Jesus and the realm of the heavenly: the Spirit from above rests on him (Jn 1:32), and angels will ascend and descend upon him (1:51). He is the one who has come down from heaven (3:13) and must be lifted back up again (3:14). Because he comes from above, he is over all and speaks on a heavenly plane (3:31-32). This theme is especially developed in two long passages which might represent editorial comment on the part of the evangelist (3:16-21 and 3:31-36). The difficulty arises because there was no device in biblical Greek to indicate where a quotation closed, so some translations put the first passage into the mouth of Jesus and the second one into the mouth of the Baptist. There is nothing wrong with that as far as the Greek text is concerned, but the discourses don't really suit these speakers. It is far more satisfactory to read them as editorial interludes, reflections on the meaning of Jesus in much the same spirit as the Prologue, tying all of the introductory material of the first three chapters together.

There is one other matter which we might turn to at this early stage of the gospel. John is often seen as being very anti-Semitic, blaming the Jews for opposition to Christ's ministry and eventually for his death. Various solutions to the problem have been suggested over the years, but the best one might be a very simple linguistic one. The Greek term, *hoi Ioudaioi*, could indeed mean "the Jews", but more strictly speaking means "the Judaeans". Certainly all Judaeans, that is people living in the province of Judaea, would be Jews but not all Jews would be Judaeans. Christ and his disciples, for instance, would be Galileans. The term, *hoi Ioudaioi*, was certainly used of Jews in general as well as of Judeans, but only by outsiders like the Romans. When a Jew wanted to refer to the whole people together, the word was "Israel". It is noteworthy that the people hail Jesus as "the King of Israel" (12:13) while Pilate the foreigner asks about the "King of the *Ioudaioi*" (18:33). Instead of condemning or vilifying the whole Jewish people, John may well only be pointing to the Israelite centre of power (Judaea, and especially Jerusalem) as also being the centre of opposition to Christ.

Throughout the rest of the sessions on the Gospel of John, the session notes will be more fully integrated with the text. Because of this there will no longer be a separate section devoted to Notes on the Text; instead, these will be incorporated into the main body of notes covering the material.

MATERIAL

Jn 1:19-3:36

AIM OF SESSION

To show how the thought of John is beginning to unfold in this section, connecting the Prologue to the main body of the Gospel.

SESSION NOTES

The Place of John The Baptist

— John the Baptist is the figure who appears at the opening and ending of this section, thus giving it a certain unity

CANA: NEW CREATION		CLEANSING OF TEMPLE:

NEWNESS

CANA: NEW CREATION

NICODEMUS: NEW BIRTH FOR NEW LIFE

CLEANSING OF TEMPLE: NEW WAY OF WORSHIP

— there were disciples of the Baptist who remained such and did not become disciples of Christ (see Act 19:1-5); the relation of the Baptist to Jesus was therefore a very important one.

1:19-27 It is made very clear that the Baptist had no messianic pretensions. The answers to the questions couldn't be more straightforward.

1:29-34 The essence of John's testimony is that Jesus is the lamb, the sacrificial animal to take away our sins. It is implied that John knew Jesus for some time before this became clear to him (v.31), and that it was only when the Spirit anointed Jesus that John knew for certain.

1:35-42 John really fulfills his role when he gets two of his disciples to follow Jesus. One of the disciples is later named (Andrew), and we should probably identify the unnamed disciple as the Beloved Disciple, from whom comes the material for this gospel.

1:43-51 If one doesn't see the humour of Jesus in John's Gospel, then it will never be seen. Jesus wins over cynical Nathanael with a compliment (v.47), amazes him with a piece of inconsequential information (v.48), only then to tell him of what really lies in store (v.50-51).

Three Stories of "Newness"

After the connection with John the Baptist, the gospel moves on to give three stories which illustrate the new reality brought in the work of Jesus: Cana illustrates the new creation, the Cleansing of the Temple shows the new meeting of God and humanity, and the conversation with Nicodemus speaks of the new birth as God's children.

The wedding feast of Cana uses water become wine as an image of how reality is transformed into something more precious and wonderful through the action of Jesus.

The idea of new creation may be hinted at in the introductory note that this occured on the third day which, if the time notes in the first chapter are all taken into consideration, is the seventh day of John's first week. In other words, the day that God originally rested has become the day that divine activity begins anew in Christ.

2:3-5 This exchange has long been a puzzle, especially concerning Jesus' reply to Mary's statement. There are obvious undercurrents here which are missed: Mary makes a statement about the lack of wine which Jesus takes up as a request which he seems to dismiss, yet Mary takes his obvious dismissal as indicating that he is about to do something. One solution is to take the idiom in verse 4 as meaning something like, "Leave this to me"; but no solution has found universal acceptance. "Woman" (Greek *guné*) seems to be the usual name of Christ for his mother in the gospel (cf. 19:26).

The second story of "newness" is the cleansing of the Temple, Christ showing the inadequacies of the old order of worship as he introduces the new.

This incident is related at the end of Christ's ministry in the synoptic gospels, but is placed by John at the beginning because for him it speaks of the whole significance of Christ's life.

The old Temple in Jerusalem was the dwelling place of God among people, the meeting place of God and humanity; Christ as the new Temple becomes the new meeting place, the new sign of God's habitation with his people.

2:14 The selling of animals was, of course, for the purpose of sacrifices to be offered in the Temple. The common currency used for day to day business had to be exchanged at exorbitant rates for special Temple currency.

2:18-23 Herod's temple was the pride of Jerusalem (see Mk 13:1), so Jesus' words must have sounded an insult as well as impossible. "The temple of his body" means that the very person of Christ is the new Temple, a theme which is developed throughout the gospel by image and overtone. It would be a mistake to read the Pauline theology of the Church as Body of Christ here; John means that human encounter with the divine is now to take place in and through the person of Jesus.

2:22 John freely admits that he did not have immediate insight into the full meaning of Christ. He portrays Jesus as a person who can be rather confusing, and yet as someone whose message is quite clear at the same time. It is faith in the risen Jesus which clarifies all.

The third story of "newness" is the conversation of Jesus with Nicodemus which speaks of new birth to eternal life.

It involves a double play in words, and Nicodemus' resulting confusion stands for the whole inability of the Judaean establishment (of which Nicodemus is a member) to understand what Christ is about.

The episode revolves around the birth *anōthen*, which Nicodemus interprets as simply being born again and so cannot accept. Jesus puts the emphasis on the other meaning of *anōthen*, from above, and so speaks of being born into the life of heaven, eternal life, which he brings.

The second play on words is on *pneuma*, which can mean wind or spirit. Jesus begins by speaking of the wind and changes to talking of the spirit while Nicodemus (as shown by verse nine) is still thinking about the wind.

3:11-12 Jesus is presented as the witness to heavenly truths because he is the one from above. John's Gospel presumes that the reader has the world view of heaven "up there" and earth "down here", and uses the distinction often. Our technological age retains enough of its mythical framework to know what John is talking about without feeling bound to his cosmic geography.

3:13-14 Just as Jesus came from the realm of the above, so on the cross he will be lifted back up towards it. The verb *hupsoō* has a double meaning of "lift up" or "exalt". The incident of the bronze serpent is to be found in Num 21:4-9.

3:16-21 An interlude by the evangelist which should not be put into the mouth of Christ. The mission of Christ is a point of decision for humanity who will either come to the light of Christ or show how deep is their attachment to darkness.

3:22-30 John's final witness is his humility in giving way to Christ. The bridegroom of verse twenty-nine is an image for the Messiah which can also be found in Mt 25 and in the Book of Revelation: as the bridegroom of those days came on the wedding day to claim his bride, so the Messiah comes in joy to claim his people. Notice that verse twenty-five makes more sense when the dispute is seen as between John's disciples and a Judaean rather than with a Jew; all of John's disciples were presumably Jews.

3:23-36 The second interlude by the evangelist (which whould not be put into the mouth of the Baptist). It summarises the first three chapters of the gospel, showing Christ to be sent from above by God to bring humanity to the plane of the eternal. As the rest of the gospel will show, he is the decision point at which people will either choose eternal life or reject it.

QUESTIONS FOR DISCUSSION

— How important is John the Baptist in this first part of the Fourth Gospel?

— Did Christ come for judgement or not?

MATERIAL AND DISCUSSION QUESTIONS FOR SESSION TWELVE

John 4-5

— One of the first problems of the early Church was whether or not to accept non-Jewish converts. What does the incident of John 4:1-42 say about this problem, especially verses 31-38?

— What does chapter five say about the relationship between Jesus and the Father?

The One of whom Moses Spoke

John 4-5

We all know that the Old Testament was in use at the time of Christ and perhaps imagine that it was collected together in some bound volume much like Bibles today. The fact is that there was no general agreement as to what made up the Old Testament until well after the Temple was destroyed, that is, until the end of the first century. When the apostles preached, they tended to use the Greek translation of the Old Testament (the Septuagint) which is basically the same as the Old Testament of a modern Catholic Bible. But the Sadducees would never have agreed with that, for they only recognised the first five books, the Torah, as being God's Word. The same would be true of that despised race of half-breeds, the Samaritans, who still treasure an ancient manuscript of those books. So then, if you wanted to speak scripturally to the whole spectrum of Jewish belief in the first century A.D., the only common ground which you could assume would be the five books of the Torah.

Reference is made to the Torah early on in John's Gospel, including one passing reference in the Prologue (1:17). The title for this session is taken from Philip's statement in 1:45, "We have found the one Moses wrote about in the Law — the prophets, too — Jesus, son of Joseph, from Nazareth." If we look at the Torah (which was commonly looked upon as written by Moses) there is only one section which we could say promises a Messiah: Deut 18:15-19. That passage promises a prophet (spokesman) for the people who will be like Moses, raised up from among the people with God's words in his mouth, who will speak out all that he is commanded, and who presents a time of decision for the people: God will make the one who refuses to listen to him answer for it. It doesn't take great imagination to see here the skeleton upon which John fleshes out his picture of Jesus as Messiah. Of course, this picture from Deuteronomy had nothing to do with the promised son of David (which is why people like the Qumran Community looked for two Messiahs, not one). John weaves together the promises associated with the Torah and the promises associated with David (through the prophets) when he shows that Jesus is the Messiah.

All of this is very relevant to the scene with the Samaritan woman. The Samaritans were expecting a Messiah, although they didn't call him that; they called him "The One Who Returns", the prophet promised by Moses. The scene with the Samaritan woman represents John at his best, taking a simple, homely scene and filling it with theological riches. Again there is a play on words here: the term "living water" was a common way of describing flowing water. So when the poor woman, weary after her long haul with the stone jars to the well, hears Jesus promise living water, her interest in him is not so much as a Saviour but as a plumber!

Then, too, there is the joyful sound of barriers crashing which echoes throughout the scene. The hatred between Jews and Samaritans vanishes from the start, as does the prejudice against women. The barrier between Jews and Samaritans was as religious as it was racial, summed up in the dispute over the one place where it was lawful to offer sacrifice: the Jews said it was Jerusalem, the Samaritans that it was Mount Gerizim. Jesus says that the one place where it is lawful to worship is in spirit and in truth. The encounter with the woman brings to the fore in Jesus his longing for souls, as can be seen in 4:31-38.

Perhaps the barriers are crossed again in the next piece, easily seen as a parallel to the cure of the centurion's servant in Lk 7:1-10. Although there are enough differences in the stories to allow us to say that these represent different incidents, the title of the man (*basilikos*, "the king's man") might indicate that he was in the service of the Roman Emperor (see Jn 19:15). If that is the case, then this story breaches the wall between Gentile and Israelite. In any event, this story is an interlude which underlines the importance of faith over signs (4:48); the man got his request because "he put his trust in the word Jesus said to him" (4:50) instead of needing the wonders on which to base his faith.

This short faith interlude is placed here because John is about to dwell on signs at great length. The Fourth Gospel is so intense in its material that the casual reader may not notice that there are very, very few incidents in it; it is a case of John milking each incident for every drop of meaning. The whole first section of the gospel is often referred to as "The Book of Signs", but from chapter five on, John handles the signs according to a pattern. Firstly, there is the sign; that is followed by a debate; and the whole incident is concluded with a teaching. If we take chapter five as an example, the sign is a miraculous cure of a paralytic. The debate centres around working on the Sabbath (5:10-16). The teaching is on the working of Jesus, Sabbath and weekday, day in and day out.

The discourse in 5:19-47 is the real point of the whole narrative. The first thing to notice is that Jesus' work depends totally on the work of the Father (5:17, 19-20). Verses nineteen and twenty are usually printed in our translations with capital letters ("Father", "the Son") but they could also be equally well printed with small letters to talk about fathers and sons in general. This could be a parable which Jesus then applies to the relationship between himself and God. A typical Johannine phrase for the Father is to be found in 5:30, "the one who sent me"; the term is meant to convey a delegate with full powers to make decisions and to speak for the sender. Throughout this monologue we can sense the two sides of Jesus' mission: firstly, that he has full authority in all matters (5:22-23, 27, 43), and secondly that he is completely faithful to the intentions of the one who has given him the mission (5:19, 30). The difference between accepting Jesus as sent from the Father and not accepting him as such is the difference between life and death. These are all themes which will be seen a few times in the Fourth Gospel.

Towards the end of this discourse, the subject of witnesses is raised. Jewish law required two witnesses on every matter, and the witnesses were often accusers as well. Jesus offers three witnesses to his mission: the first is the Baptist, whose witness is nearly dismissed as unimportant (5:33-36); the Father himself is given as a witness, though one which Jesus' opponents refuse to hear (5:37-38); the final witness, who is the accuser, is the most ironic of all — Moses, to whom the Judaeans look for the guiding light of their lives, is both witness and accuser for those who study him but do not listen to him. That should also remind us to look at what this chapter says about the work

Jews and Samaritans agreed there was only one place to worship; they just disagreed where it was.

of Christ in light of Deut 18:15-19. When we do, we should see that it fits perfectly, even to the dire consequences for those who refuse to listen to the messenger who brings the complete message of God.

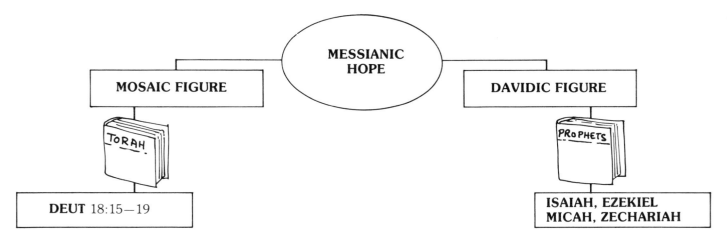

MOSAIC FIGURE

DAVIDIC FIGURE

DEUT 18:15—19

ISAIAH, EZEKIEL
MICAH, ZECHARIAH

MATERIAL

John 4-5

AIM OF SESSION

To place the messianism of the Fourth Gospel against the background of Deut 18; to highlight the different strands to be found in chapters four and five.

SESSION NOTES

"The One of Whom Moses Spoke"

— this phrase (taken from 1:45) implies that the Torah promised a Messiah, whereas most messianic hope is built upon the promise to David, especially as developed in the prophetic books

— the only section of the Torah which develops a hope for a figure in the future is Deut 18:15-19 which promises that a prophet like Moses will arise in the future

— this passage has an added significance when it is remembered that some divisions of Yahwistic belief (the Sadducees and Samaritans) would not necessarily accept the prophetic writings as God's Word but would accept the Torah

The figure promised in Deut 18 has certain features which are employed to the full by the Fourth Gospel's portrait of Jesus:

— he arises from the people of Israel

— God's message is in his mouth

— he speaks all that he is commanded

— the one who refuses to listen will be held responsible

The Samaritan Incident

— there was a deep division between Jew and Samaritan

— the rabbis taught that all Samaritans were "unclean", that is, that to have anything to do with them would make one unfit for normal social activity, especially for worship; this held doubly true for Samaritan women

— the Samaritans were worshippers of Yahweh and held the Torah to be the inspired Word of God

4:6-9 The scene is given a very human setting. It is no accident that the gospel which portrays Jesus most explicitly as Son of God also shows his fullest humanity; here he is tired and thirsty. The Samaritan woman uses the term *Ioudaios* in another outsider's way, to refer to any Israelite whether Judaean or not.

4:10 When Jesus mentions "living water", it is the same term which would commonly be used for flowing water, a misunderstanding which the Samaritan woman is quick to hold on to.

4:11-14 An ancient tradition held that Jacob's well overflowed for twenty years. Whereas we might well consider such a phenomenon a nuisance, in the arid land of Palestine this was a sign of overwhelming blessings. Jesus tells the woman that the fountain which he is offering won't just go on for a generation, but for eternity.

4:15-19 Johannine humour comes fast and furious. Firstly, the woman's misunderstanding is underlined, showing that she is more concerned about the weight of stone water jars than about eternal life. Then Jesus exposes her extraordinary marital situation (the maximum number of men that she could have had as husbands in succession was three; she was two over the limit). And then she deftly changes the subject. John seems to have enjoyed telling this story.

4:20-24 One bone of contention between Jew and Samaritan was the proper place of worship. Both agreed that the Torah only allowed for one place for sacrifice — the Jew held that it was in Jerusalem and the Samaritan that it was on Mount Gerizim. Jesus says that the place to worship the Father is "in spirit and in truth"

4:25-26 The Samaritan hope of a Messiah was referred to as "the one who comes", echoed in the phrasing here. Jesus' answer is literally translated, "I am, I who speak to you." For the significance of "I am", see the next session.

4:27-38 The disciples are scandalised, but say nothing. Jesus speaks to them about the great harvest which is ready for the reaping.

4:39-43 Perhaps this is a final touch of humour in the incident. The woman's importance as the one who knew Jesus had to fade as people began to know him for themselves.

The Faith Interlude
— This story, reminiscent of Luke 7,1-10, highlights that faith is more important than miracles.

— It serves as an introduction to a part of the gospel where a few incidents are handled in depth.

The Paralytic
— the first part of the gospel is often called "The Book of Signs" because of the limitation of miracles to this half of the work

— there is an underlying pattern in many of these incidents:

— the sign (often a miraculous event)

— a debate among the onlookers, or of the onlookers with Jesus

— a discourse by Jesus which brings out the meaning of the sign

5:1-9 The sign is the healing of a paralytic. The explanation of the curative property of the waters sometimes found in verses three and four is not found in the best Greek manuscripts and is undoubtedly a later addition.

5:10-15 The debate is about work, especially working on the Sabbath. The remark in 5:14 reflects the biblical outlook that sin and suffering are connected (although not in every case; see Jn 9:2-3).

5:16-20 The debate leads into the discourse on the work of Jesus. He justifies what he does on the Sabbath by indicating that he must be at work in the same way that his Father is at work. Verses nineteen and twenty might be read as speaking about fathers and sons in general as a type of parable.

5:21-30 Reaction to Jesus is itself a bringing of judgement. See Deut 18:19. Calling the Father "the one who sent me" shows Jesus' full authority.

5:31-47 Jewish law required two witnesses to substantiate any case, and the witnesses often acted as prosecutors as well. Jesus tells the Judaeans that they have three witnesses to him: John the Baptist (5:33-35), the Father (5:36-38), and Moses (5:39-47). The last is also a reminder of the passage in Deuteronomy.

— One of the first problems of the early Church was whether or not to accept non-Jewish converts. What does the incident of John 4:1-42 say about this problem, especially verses 31-38?

— What does chapter five say about the relationship between Jesus and the Father?

MATERIAL AND DISCUSSION QUESTIONS FOR SESSION THIRTEEN

John 6

— Most commentators read this chapter as eucharistic — especially verses 48 to 59; what facets of the Eucharist are highlighted here?

— If one reads this chapter non-eucharistically, it makes certain comments on the place of Christ in the life of the believer; what are some of these comments?

Thirteenth Session
The Bread of Life

John 6

The Old Testament outlook wasn't always exactly "supernatural". Take the whole area of blessings, for instance. If God blessed you in the Old Testament, you knew it, your neighbours knew it, and your bank manager knew it; for the blessings of God, at least in some of the Old Testament, would be abundance and prosperity. The blessings promised in Deuteronomy 29:1-14, for instance, cover fertility of the flocks and produce of the fields and replenishment of the larder and even a favourable balance of trade!

But the Old Testament also knew that you could have a lot and not be happy with it; glimpses of that can be caught in Mic 6:14 or Hag 1:6. This was a sign that something was wrong between people and God, that although there was abundance, or at least sufficiency, God's blessing wasn't in it and so it didn't bring satisfaction. The opposite could hold true as well, that one could be satisfied with relatively little, especially if it were received from a very good person. One ancient interpretation of Ruth 2:14 was that Boaz was such a good man that when hungry Ruth ate one grain from his hand, it was enough to fill her up. This same idea of very little being enough because it comes with God's blessing can be seen in II Kings 4:42-44, although here some miraculous multiplication of the bread and grain is implied.

Of course, if abundance of goods and satisfaction from them were signs of God's blessings, they would certainly abound in the days of Messiah. the popular idea of a messianic banquet (especially in terms of a wedding banquet) is used a few times in the gospels, and nowhere more than in the narratives of the multiplication of the loaves and fishes.

The importance of the multiplication of loaves in the gospel traditions can be seen from the fact that it is related six times in four gospels, and is the only incident apart from the Passion and Resurrection to receive such attention. It is definitely treated as miraculous, and all the narratives as well are imbued with overtones. The Fourth Gospel, by means of the discourse, brings out the meaning even more fully.

The numbers in the Scriptures are often meant to be very significant, as the strange passage in Mk 8:18-21 indicates, as the repetition of threes and sevens and forties should show. The numbers here are five (five loaves, five thousand men) and twelve (twelve baskets of leftovers) and both numbers have overtones which relate to the people of Israel. Multiples of five were common in divisions of the people (as in Ex 18:21 or Deut 1:15), and of course five itself was the number of scrolls in the basic Scripture of Israel, the Torah. Twelve is an even more obvious number, the number of tribes in Israel and the number

If God blessed you in the Old Testament, you knew it, your neighbors knew it, and your bank manager knew it.

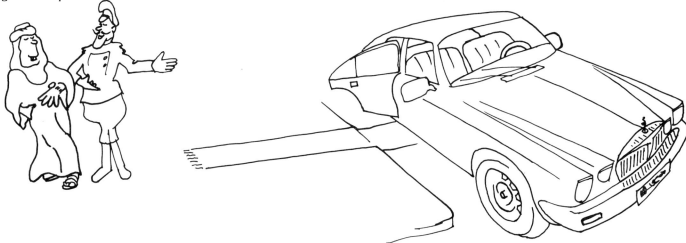

of patriarchs from which they were descended. So the numbers tell us that this event was meant for the whole people of God, of which the group present was a small representation.

Far more familiar are the eucharistic resonances of this chapter; they are not just in the discourse, but in the narration of the miracle itself. Verse eleven uses the vocabulary of the Lord's Supper when it says that Jesus took, blessed (the Greek word is a verbal form of "Eucharist") and gave the loaves. John adds another eucharistic term in verse twelve when Jesus tells the disciples to gather the fragments, since this mark of respect formed part of the eucharistic action of the early Church as we know from the *Didache*.

The incident of Jesus' walking on the water is a divine manifestation. Most of the miracles of Christ in all of the gospels show his concern for people more than anything else; but from time to time his divine mastery of the forces of nature is displayed by his control of the sea (as in Mk 4:35-41 or Mt 14:22-33). Perhaps this is linked to the Hebrew distrust of the sea and healthy respect for its dangers.

In this incident, Jesus identifies himself with a phrase generally translated, "It is I"; the Greek is *egō eimi*, literally, "I am." The phrase is one widely used in John's Gospel, especially in connection with various statements of Christ such as "I am the vine", "I am the way, the truth and the life", and "I am the bread of life." Certainly the phrase could be one of simple identification ("It's me", as in Jn 9:9), but most scholars are reluctant to leave it at that. The *egō* is too emphatic; it is unnecessary in most of the places where it occurs. So the common approach is that this phrase is meant to echo the "I AM" that lies behind the divine name Yahweh (see Ex 3:14). Certainly that would explain the strange reaction of the Judaeans in Jn 18:6; when Jesus says *egō eimi* to identify himself the chief priests and Pharisees fall to the ground in veneration of the divine name.

The discourse is identified in 6:59 as originating in a synagogue instruction in Capernaum; since such an instruction would be based on and Old Testament text, the discourse is probably to be related to Ex 16:4-15. The discourse in Jn 6 also includes the debate about the sign and its meaning.

Catholics tend to read the whole discourse as referring to the Eucharist, as do most non-Catholic commentators. There is another way to read this according to some of the Church fathers. They also use this discourse to refer to the centrality of the person of Jesus to the believer. Perhaps the first part of the discourse might be best read from this viewpoint; but it is impossible to exclude the eucharistic references of the discourse from 6:52 on. The importance of the teaching of chapter six receives its exclamation point from the rejection of Jesus by many of his former disciples and by the more emphatic act of Jesus in silently letting them go. This is also the place for Peter to act as spokesman for the Twelve with the Johannine profession of faith (6:68-69).

MATERIAL

John 6

AIM OF SESSION

To investigate different overtones in the Johannine treatment of the Feeding of the Five Thousand, especially the eucharistic overtones; to examine briefly the meaning of John's "I am".

SESSION NOTES

The Miracle of the Loaves and Fishes

— this miracle made enough of an impression to be retold six times in the four gospels.

— the miracle depends on two expectations of the blessings of God:

— that they bring material abundance;

— that God's gifts will satisfy human longing.

101

NOT THE MANNA IN THE DESERT		MY FLESH, REAL FOOD MY BLOOD, REAL DRINK
	I AM THE BREAD OF LIFE	
THIS BREAD GIVES ETERNAL LIFE		MY FLESH FOR THE LIFE OF THE WORLD

Abundance and satisfaction were especially expected in the day of the Messiah.

— sometimes captured in the image of a "messianic banquet" for all God's people

— the "messianic banquet" appears at times in the gospel as a wedding banquet, the wedding of the Messiah to his people

6:4 The first eucharistic overtone of this passage is its indication that the feast of Passover was near, the time associated with the Last Supper.

6:10 The 5,000 men and five loaves use a number associated with divisions of the people, the number of books of the Law and the number of books in the psalter. One implication is that this is a representative group of God's people.

6:11-12 Jesus' actions are eucharistic: taking, blessing and giving, seeing that the fragments are gathered.

6:13 Twelve is another number with overtones: twelve tribes of Israel, twelve patriarchs from whom they trace their descent.

6:14-15 The people do not miss the messianic overtones of the incident and want to crown Jesus as Messiah according to their idea of what a Messiah should be. Jesus does not want that type of messianism.

The Great "I AM"

— the mastery of Jesus over nature is often shown in the gospels as mastery over the sea

— most other miracles are more concerned with the needs of people than with displaying Jesus' power

— The Hebrew mentality had a distrust of the sea with its sudden storms and hidden dangers (Ps 107:23-32).

— In this passage, Jesus identifies himself with a phrase often on his lips in the Fourth Gospel: *egó eimi*, "I am", "It is I".

— at times it is a simple identification (Jn 9:9)

— usually more theological: "I am the vine", "I am the resurrection"

— thought to be an echo of the divine name Yahweh; see Ex 3:14 and Jn 18:6

The Bread of Life Discourse

— this is taken from a synagogue teaching (6:59), probably based on a passage about the manna (Ex 16:4-15)

— it combines the element of debate and discourse concerning the sign (the Feeding of the Five Thousand)

— part of the discourse could be read to show the centrality of the person of Jesus to the life of the believer (6:25-51)

— the second part of the discourse is eucharistic and gives a eucharistic flavour to the whole

6:26-27 Jesus insists that people do not identify God's blessings with material benefits but look for the real gifts which God can give.

6:32-33 The bread from heaven is not to be identified with the past giving of manna and Moses, but with the Father who is giving still.

6:35 Another *egō eimi*, repeated in 6:41,48 and 51. Jesus says to feed on him is to have eternal life.

6:41-42 The Judaeans are introduced; they reject the heavenly origin of Jesus which is so central to understanding his mission in John's gospel.

6:44-51 The difference between the gift of God in the manna in the desert and the gift of God in Jesus is eternal life. Verse fifty-one is reminiscent of Lk 22:19, "This is my body, given for you."

6:52-58 This is the explicitly eucharistic section, and possibly verse fifty-one should be included in it. Verse fifty-five could not be more emphatic; it is real food and real drink that are being spoken of. The bread of life is essential for eternal life.

6:60-66 The sadness of rejection does not make Jesus go back on his teaching. Verse sixty-three again stresses the difference between a materialistic approach and one which will bring eternal life.

6:67-71 The Twelve are faithful and make a confession of faith through Peter (as in Mt 16:16). Yet even the Twelve are not entirely without their deserters, as Judas was to later prove.

QUESTIONS FOR DISCUSSION

— Most commentators read this chapter as eucharistic — especially verses 48 to 59; what facets of the Eucharist are highlighted here?

— If one reads this chapter non-eucharistically, it makes certain comments on the place of Christ in the life of the believer; what are some of these comments?

MATERIAL AND DISCUSSION QUESTIONS FOR SESSION FOURTEEN

John 7-8
— Some false ideas are expressed by the people in these chapters; give some of them with the true statements which they deny.

— Are Christians the children of Abraham? Look at Galatians chapter four when considering your answer.

Jesus at the Feast of Tabernacles

John 7-8

The sixth chapter of John's gospel was set in Galilee, but the chapter before was a healing done in Jerusalem. Whereas the first three gospels speak of a ministry conducted in Galilee and only mention one journey during that ministry to Jerusalem (for the final scenes of the gospel), the fourth gospel shows most of its activity in Jerusalem and its surroundings. Chapter seven continues on the debate and the conflict arising from the healing in chapter five (see 7:21-24), stressing the growing tensions between Jesus and the people of Jerusalem, especially the authorities.

The timing of the episode gives it its flavour: the feast of Tabernacles (or Succoth, or Booths). It was one of the three "pilgrimage feasts" of the Old Testament when Jerusalem was crowded with pilgrims (the others were Passover and Pentecost). The Old Testament references (Lev 23:33-44; Deut 16:13-17) don't tell us too much on their own about the feast except that it was an autumn festival, during which the Israelites lived in booths, and at which there was to be much rejoicing. From elsewhere, we can add details of more relevance to this passage of the gospel.

Tabernacles was in part a celebration of the Temple (see II Mac 1:18). The Temple was illuminated for the occasion with great lights, and there was even dancing with lights at night in the court. Another notable part of the festival celebrations in the Temple was a procession with water through Jerusalem to the Temple where it was poured out in libation on the altar for the seven days of the feast. This could be considered a prayer for the winter rains, made during this harvest festival to ensure the harvest for the following year. When the Jews made their solemn assembly for the feast of Tabernacles, rain was on everyone's mind.

At the feast of tabernacles rain was on everyone's mind.

The two key statements which Jesus makes in these chapters get their impact from this festival setting. The first is about water and thirst, in 7:37-38. Exactly how this should be read is a matter of dispute, and the late medieval verse numbering adds to the difficulty. This would seem the most reasonable way to read it:

> If anyone is thirsty, he should come to me,
> and believing in me, let him drink,
> just as the Scripture said.
> From inside him shall run
> rivers of living water.

The Scripture reference then would be to drinking from Jesus, not to the rivers of living water; the Old Testament passages which might be referred to could include Is 12:3; Joel 4:18; Prov 9:5 and Ps 42:2-3. The reference to there being no Spirit as yet (7:39) is John's way of saying that Jesus was so full of the Spirit that he had a monopoly on the market until he handed the Spirit over to his followers in the cross and resurrection.

The other key statement is in 8:12: Jesus is the light of the world. Light, too, would have been a very prominent feature in the Jerusalem celebrations of tabernacles, so it is appropriate that Christ makes this claim, also on the last day of the celebrations. This is one of many reasons for saying that the charming incident of 7:53-8:11 is not really in its proper place, for it would mean that the festival was over. The major reasons for placing the incident of the women caught in adultery elsewhere are linguistic: the thing just isn't written in John's vocabulary or style. It seems really to belong to the synoptics,

perhaps after Lk 21:38 where a family of manuscripts have placed it. It is, of course, part of inspired Scripture no matter where it is finally placed.

Throughout this section there is much talk about origins, especially about the origins of Jesus. The Fourth Gospel uses this as an approach to the rejection of Jesus by the people: they couldn't accept him because they couldn't face up to the fact that he really came from above, and that his earthly origins just didn't matter. The only sense in which his human background is important is that he can be said to be the prophet raised from among the Jews' own kin (as in Deut 18:15-19), the precise sticking point for the non-believers.

Other questions of origins are also prominent in the passage, or, more precisely, questions of descent. A burning question of New Testament times (hardly smoldering in our own) was "Who inherits the promises to Abraham?" Paul, as we saw, had his own approach (see session nine), and answers are hinted at elsewhere in the New Testament (as in Lk 3:8). The problem was that Abraham's descendants were to receive the fulfilment of all God's promises, so how could non-believing Jews be excluded from the blessings of Christ or, more to the point, how could believing non-Jews profit from the promised Messiah? In short, the answer is that physical descent has little to do with the promise; it is spiritual descent that matters. This is what lies at the heart of the argument in 8:31-59, an argument difficult to follow at times. The final thrust of the discussion is that, as important as he is, even Abraham rejoices because of Jesus, the great "I AM" (8:56-58).

MATERIAL

John 7-8

AIM OF SESSION

To situate this passage against the background of the feast of Tabernacles.

The Setting of the Scene in the Gospel

— the multiplication of the loaves and fishes is placed in Galilee, where most of the happenings of the first three gospels take place

— these gospels tell only of one journey to Jerusalem during the public ministry of Christ, before the events of Holy Week

— John's Gospel puts much more of its action in Jerusalem and surrounding areas, highlighting the tension between Jesus and the Judean authorities

— when Jesus returns to Jerusalem, it is still in the aftermath to the sign he worked there previously (chapter five; see Jn 7:21-24)

7:1 Keeping to the suggestion of translating *Ioudaioi* as "Judaeans", this sentence makes perfect sense: "And after these things, Jesus was going around in Galilee; for he did not want to go around in Judaea since the Judeans were looking to kill him." "Jews" were to be found in Galilee as well, but "Judaeans" could be more easily avoided.

7:2 The thought would occur to every devout Jew to go up to Jerusalem for the feast of Tabernacles.

7:3-9 The Lord's brothers could refer to members of his extended family, most likely cousins, and this is the usual interpretation by Catholic and Orthodox Christians. They were sceptical of Jesus' claims during his life, although some of them at least seemed to have changed their minds after the resurrection (see Acts 1:14). James, who was called "the brother of the Lord", was head of the Jerusalem Church until his death in 62 A.D.

105

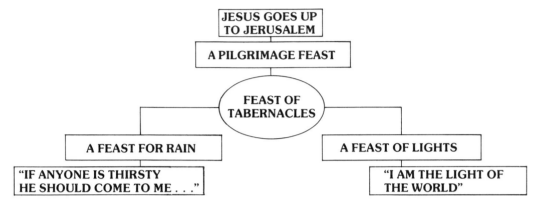

JESUS GOES UP TO JERUSALEM

A PILGRIMAGE FEAST

FEAST OF TABERNACLES

A FEAST FOR RAIN

"IF ANYONE IS THIRSTY HE SHOULD COME TO ME . . ."

A FEAST OF LIGHTS

"I AM THE LIGHT OF THE WORLD"

The Feast of Tabernacles

— this festival, also called "Booths" or its Hebrew name *Succoth*, was an autumn harvest festival, during which the Jews made a pilgrimage to the Temple in Jerusalem (Lev 23:33-44; Deut 16:13-17)

— in the time of Christ, much of the celebration centred around the Temple:

— the Temple was decorated with lights and in one of its courts, dances with lights took place at night.

— water also had an important place; for seven days there was a solemn procession with water from Siloam which was poured out after on the altar.

— possibly linked to its nature as a harvest festival, the prayer for the winter rains was made at the time of Tabernacles; these rains were essential for the produce of the coming year

— Christ uses both of these festival images to speak of himself during the festival, on the last and greatest day:

— he is the answer to the longing of everyone's thirst (7:37-38)

— he is the light of the world (8:12)

— During the debates of this section, many statements are made about Jesus' origins. For John, no one can understand Christ without realising that he belongs to the realm of the heavenly, that he comes from above; to accept Christ is to become part of that realm (3:3).

7:10-13 Jesus arrives in Jerusalem to find the debate about him is continuing. Is he good, or is he misleading the crowds?

7:15-17 A question of origins is raised: from where does Christ's teaching come? Just as the scribes of Jesus' day pointed to other teachers as their authority, so Christ points to the Father from whom his teaching comes.

7:19-26 The former sign in Jerusalem was the start of proceedings against Christ in John (5:16-18). The drama continues from where it had ended in chapter five.

7:27 Another question of origins arises; but the crowd is doubly mistaken. Firstly, they don't realise that Jesus is from above eternally; they think that his beginnings are in Galilee. Secondly, the Messiah is to be from among their own kin (Deut 18:15-19).

7:28-29 "The One who sent me" is the real answer to Jesus' origins.

7:30-36 While the debate continues, the Pharisees try to take action; but such an important cosmic event as the death of Jesus is not at the whims of merely human plans. It is reserved to an appointed "hour", before which nothing can happen. When Jesus returns to the realm of the above, those who insist on being earthly can never follow.

7:37-39 Everyone's mind during this feast of Tabernacles is on the need for water, so Jesus chooses to describe himself as the answer to thirst. The quotation should read: "If anyone is thirsty, he should come to me; and believing in me, let him drink, just as the Scripture said. From inside him shall run rivers of living water." Quotations concerned with satisfying thirst from Jesus would include Is 12:3, Joel 4:18; Prov 9:5 and Ps 42:2-3. John is not making a precise doctrinal statement when he says that there was no Spirit yet, just that Jesus was so full of the Spirit that he had to give the Spirit in the cross and resurrection before we could speak of the Spirit in anyone else.

7:40-52 Back to the questions of origins again. The opponents of Jesus are so blinded by appearances that anyone who speaks up for Christ is labelled "another Galilean".

7:53-8:11 A beautiful passage, and part of the gospel traditions about Jesus, but it doesn't belong here. Some manuscripts place it in Luke's Gospel, where it would seem to fit better. One problem about putting it here is that it would end the feast of Tabernacles in chapter seven, whereas the language of the feast is still being spoken in chapter eight.

8:12 Jesus invokes the illumination of the Temple and dancing with torches when he calls himself the light of the world.

8:18-19 The Pharisees cannot understand Jesus because they have no knowledge of the Father. The only way to know the Father fully, however, is by knowing Jesus.

8:21-26 The contrast is again made between Jesus who is "from above" and the unbelieving Judaeans who are "from below".

8:28 Lifting Jesus on the cross is going to raise him back into the realm of the above in John's Gospel. John is highly aware of the cross as the triumph of love and obedience, not as the human defeat of Jesus (see the notes on 3:11-12 and 3:13-14 in Session Eleven.) This is also the moment when Christ will be seen as *egō eimi*, the great "I AM".

8:30 The picture in John is never of universal rejection of Jesus, but that many became believers. The picture of the whole population of Palestine calling for Christ's death in Pilate's courtyard is most unbiblical.

Abraham's Family

— one problem for the early Church (which had rapid growth among the Gentiles) was the question of how can non-Jews inherit the promises made to Abraham and to his descendants.

— some extremists wanted to make the Gentiles converts to Judaism first, and then Christians; this was rejected by the Church elders and apostles in Acts 15:1-29

— the problem is reflected elsewhere in the New Testament (e.g., Paul's Letter to the Galatians and Luke 3:8)

— all solutions agree that physical descent is not what guarantees inheriting the promises to Abraham; the relationship must be stronger, linked to imitation of what Abraham did

8:31-32 The believing Judaeans are told that they must continue in the word of Jesus to become free; as good as their belief up to now might be, it was not enough. The concept of remaining (Greek: *menō*, to remain, continue, abide, live on) will appear again and again in the Fourth Gospel, especially in the Last Supper Discourses.

8:33-36 The highly nationalistic Judaeans will suffer no slur on their freedom. But the freedom of which Jesus speaks is the freedom of the children of God from sin, which makes the Judaeans slaves.

8:37-41 Although he accepts their claim to physical descendancy from Abraham, Jesus does not accept that the Judaeans (who are trying to kill him) can claim that Abraham is their father if Abraham is not imitated.

8:41-43 A new approach is tried: "God is our Father!" But this claim, too, is rejected by Jesus.

8:44-47 If actions are the criterion (and they are!), then Satan is the only one who is father to those who reject Jesus. To reject Jesus is to reject truth and to throw in one's lot with the father of lies.

8:48-51 The (now) unbelieving Judaeans reject Christ as a Samaritan (another mistake about origins) and possessed (thus accounting for his ability to perform signs and wonders). Jesus affirms his obedience to the Father and again states the reward for those who keep his Word.

8:52-56 The discussion returns to "our father Abraham". Jesus returns to his Father, God, and says that even Abraham found joy in Jesus.

8:57-59 Jesus states that he is the eternal "I AM" and the crowd try to stone him for blasphemy.

QUESTIONS FOR DISCUSSION

— Some false ideas about Jesus are expressed by the people in these chapters; give some of them with the true statements which they deny.

— Are Christians the children of Abraham? Look at Galatians chapter four when considering your answer.

MATERIAL AND DISCUSSION QUESTIONS FOR SESSION FIFTEEN

John 9-10

— Chapter nine makes faith equal to sight. What does it say about blindness?

— What is Christ saying about himself when he refers to Shepherd and sheep? Look at Ezek 34, II Sam 7:8, Mic 5:1-3, Psalms 23,80 and 100.

Fifteenth Session
Blindness and Sight

John 9-10

Although the Scripture is a library with a vast variety of types of writing, the most outstanding and least appreciated of its methods of communicating is that of telling a story. The insensitivity of modern readers to story is shown by the way that the message of "Adam and Eve" was taken to heart (at least in some form) as long as the story was believed to be historical; but as soon as the archaeologists gave up their search for the fossilised apple core on the banks of the Tigris, the whole teaching of Genesis 2-3 tended to be rolled up like an old newspaper and thrown into the bin as "only a story".

The human person, however, is not so sophisticated as to be able to live in a world of mathematical equations without story. Our world operates on story to entertain, to inform, to reason, to explain. Logical reasoning and statistical studies are grand, as far as they go. But they are restricted, kept to the safe organised civilisation of our most rational intellect. But a story can go much farther: it can stroll through the mountain ranges of our experience, hack through the thick undergrowth of our emotions, swim against the strong currents of our bigotries, and present us with treasures of truth which would never be discovered in the organised streets of our logic. Shakespeare might have written a short essay on how the drive for power dehumanises; instead he wrote Macbeth and his message still resonates after essays are forgotten.

Exactly how story operates is one of the unanswered mysteries, but there are certain insights which can be very useful for an appreciation of story in Scripture. The story is easily seen as a movement from one state to another. How it makes that movement gives us the meaning of the story. The characters in a story are what involve the reader: some characters we love, some we dislike, some we identify ourselves with. It is the characters in a story that make us realise that the whole point is not some abstract truth; they shake us into acknowledging that the story is about us.

The details of a story can also prepare us to see the significance and application of a story, especially if those details become symbolic. In *Lord of the Flies*, to take one example, the group who start their own society are choirboys since

choirboys, with their Christmas card collars and cherub appearance, strike chords of innocent childhood in many a reader's imagination. The details of biblical stories, too, can sometimes be intended to remind the readers of something which will point them to the heart of the subject.

We differ from the original audiences of biblical narratives in that we have a concern with history which is nearly neurotic. The Scriptures are free from such neuroses. Sometimes it is very important that something in Scripture is historical alright, such as the Resurrection of Jesus. But if we take the time to examine the accounts of even something as central and important as the Resurrection, we have to admit that the gospel writers were not concerned with giving a uniform, official account, nor even accounts that could be conveniently harmonised. The lesson is that where modern concern with a story is with *facts*, the biblical story is concerned with *truth*. And truth, despite modern prejudices, is something which can never be imprisoned by mere facts.

Even the historical concern of Scripture is different to our own. Our historical questions are ones like where, who, how, and when. The only historical questions which Scripture really knows is why, and it always looks for the answer to that question in God.

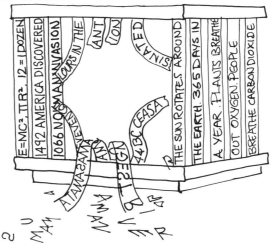

Truth is something which can never be imprisoned by mere facts.

Chapter nine of the Fourth Gospel gives us a tremendous opportunity to examine the method of biblical story. It seems to be a unit in itself, not always expressing things in quite the way that we would expect of the Fourth Gospel. It is certainly the finest example in John of a story being allowed to speak the message on its own without a following discourse.

The movement of the story is three-fold. Firstly, there is the simple movement from blindness to sight, the type of movement which we are familiar with from many stories in the first three gospels. But this movement is loaded with details: the disciples' automatic association of suffering and personal sin; the identification of Jesus as the light of the world; the anointing of the eyes and washing in the pool called Sent. The story would have reminded its original hearers of baptismal "illumination" and cleansing. But there's more. The second movement is the interrogation and expulsion from the synagogue. Certainly this, too, would have sounded familiar, since expulsion from the synagogue was a reality which converts to Christianity would have had to face (although from exactly what date is a matter of dispute). But the third movement is the one which scores the goal: the former blind man moves from ignorance of Jesus to acknowledgement of him to worship of him. And with this last movement, all the pieces fall into place. And what blindness really is, and what sin really is, becomes clear in the shining light of Christ.

The connection between the story of chapter nine and the discourses of chapter ten is only a loose one. It is generally not referred to by the ordinary reader, nor by the use of these chapters in the Lectionary. But the connection is there. Just as chapter nine tells the story of one person's discovery of Jesus, so the discourses of ten speak of the intimate relationship between Jesus and his sheep, one of mutual recognition and attachment, one that will cost the Good Shepherd his life. Then there is the question of those who refuse to follow the Shepherd or even to understand him. The gospel considers that problem in the light of faith in Jesus as a gift and the sheep themselves being a gift to Jesus from the Father. Rejection of Jesus for John is not some well-meaning questioning or tolerant indifference: in the Fourth Gospel, rejecting Jesus is picking up stones to get rid of him. John's Jesus is such a strong figure that one is either drawn to him or repulsed by him. One gets the feeling that if John were to see our society and the indifference which very good people can have towards Christ, John might have some very hard questions about the image and type of Christ which we Christians are presenting to the world.

The tensions and pace of the gospel are increasing, and the group should feel something of the dangers into which Jesus is moving. But it is not that the author of the Fourth Gospel is writing a story which he knows must come to a climax in the cross, and therefore stretches its shadow back across the story. No, John's concern is to tell how the Word sounded more and more clearly in the world of humanity, and the more clearly it sounded, the more people showed how they hated the sound of it. The more Jesus revealed himself, the more repulsive he was to those who rejected him; and when he revealed himself fully, he was the complete victim of all the hatred and rejection in the human heart.

MATERIAL

John 9-10

AIM OF SESSION

To discover the workings of story in Scripture, especially in the context of the story of the blind man in John chapter nine.

SESSION NOTES

The Bible Teaches Through Story

— the basic movement of a story is its main method for teaching truth.

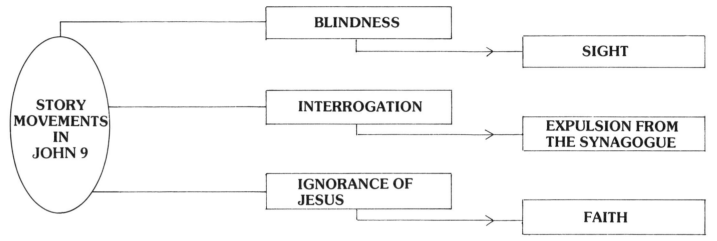

— the Bible often uses story to present God's message, because it is a much more powerful means of communication than mere logical argument.

— besides movement, story uses many other tools to present its insights:

— the characters of a story involve the reader, especially the characters with whom the reader can identify

— the details of a story can be symbolic, making the reader think of his own experience, or linking the story to realities outside the story

— biblical stories can use all of the ordinary tricks of the trade in story-telling: humour, surprise, emotion, allusion, exaggeration, and so on

For most biblical stories, history is not a concern; neither should it preoccupy the attentions of the modern biblical reader.

— modern man has an unhealthy concern with facts, but the ancients knew that truth is bigger than facts

— that some happenings in the Bible are historical is important (such as the death and resurrection of Jesus); even then, the details of what happened are judged irrelevant by the Scriptures

— when Scripture does examine history, it asks a different historical question; our historical question are "Who?", "Where?", "When?"; the only historical question that the Bible knows is "Why?", and the answer to that is always found in God

The Man Born Blind

Chapter nine provides an excellent example of a biblical story which gives a sublime teaching.

In some ways it is not as characteristic of the Fourth Gospel as other parts; it could even be seen as included in the later edition of the Fourth Gospel which is the one included in the New Testament (see Session Eighteen).

The movement of the story occurs in three shorter movements; very often the best way to approach a biblical story is to break it down into the smaller movements to see what is being said at each stage.

111

The first movement of the story is one from blindness to sight, and is filled with many overtones and allusions.

9:1-2 A child born blind must have seemed such a calamity that it was nothing less than a judgement of God upon the family. We know that the Book of Job should have eliminated this way of thinking, but the reaction of the disciples shows that it was still very much around, as it is today.

9:5 Against a background of blindness, Christ identifies himself as the light of the world, thus setting the stage for the real meaning of this sign to appear. This, by the way, is *not* an *egō eimi* statement, whereas that phrase is found in 9:9. The unusual use of this phrase alone might set off this chapter from the rest of the gospel.

9:6-7 The word for anointing is the same root as the word for "Christ", and the name for the pool (Siloam, which means "Sent") also reminds the reader of the one sent by the Father. The overtones of being united to Christ (in Baptism) are hardly accidental.

The second movement of the story is from sight to being expelled from the synagogue; expulsion from the synagogue was often a direct result in later years of being a convert to Christ. Acts of the Apostles gives a wealth of evidence that the early Christians made great use of the synagogues for as long as they were permitted.

9:8-17 The wonder creates a bit of a stir, which brings the blind man into the centre of the spotlight. the debate brings out the sides which people are taking about Jesus; but the blind man is still unclear about his own position on Jesus, even though he knows that Jesus has done something wonderful for him.

9:18-34 The humour and banter of these verses should be enjoyed. The parents are overly-concerned about their own status, but the blind man stands his ground. He sees that experience does not tally with the official position which the Judaeans have adopted about Jesus. His insights earns him excommunication.

The third movement brings the story to its conclusion and draws out the meaning; the blind man comes to worship Christ, and the Pharisees reject him in their self-righteousness.

9:38 The word for worship in Greek is somewhat ambiguous, since it can also mean to prostrate oneself; here there can be little doubt that John means to emphasise the divinity of Christ in the blind man's action.

9:34-41 The ancients apparently thought of sight as light entering a person through the eyes (see Lk 11:34). True blindness is when a person so closes his eyes that the Light of the World is not allowed in.

The Good Shepherd

Shepherd is a very rich term in the Old Testament, often being applied to the king as shepherd of his people; although this identification might be connected with King David the shepherd boy, it is a common one in the Ancient Near East in places that have no connection with David.

Far more memorable in the Old Testament are the passages wherein God is called Shepherd; some of these are referred to in the second discussion question.

Jesus describes himself as a shepherd who owns the sheep; against the Old Testament background, this forms one of the strongest claims in the mouth of Jesus to his divinity, and the reaction in 10:31-39 shows that it does not go unnoticed.

This section is loosely connected with the story in chapter nine by its emphasis on the relationship between Jesus and each member of his flock.

10:7-10 Undoubtedly a strange image, and one which some scholars have tried to explain away in various ways. Yet, as it stands, it makes a point, that Jesus is the only legitimate way into the flock of God.

10:11-18 The image changes and strengthens: Jesus claims to be a shepherd who owns the sheep and whose concern for them is limitless. Although most of the New Testament views the resurrection as the action of the Father to ratify all of the words and actions of Jesus, 10:17-18 gives another perspective (and one with which older members of the group will be much more at home).

10:22-23 The feast of the Dedication is probably only mentioned to tell us that the scene is a winter one; the festival is better known today by its Hebrew name of Hanukkah.

10:30 There is a great temptation to see in this verse the traditional Jewish identification of Yahweh as "the One". In any case, the claims of Jesus lead to a violent reaction, stoning for blasphemy.

10:40 Jesus leaves Judaean territory, and continues his activity in safety. The fact that a great number of people come to faith is something which the fourth gospel keeps repeating, quietly but consistently.

QUESTIONS FOR DISCUSSION

— Chapter nine makes faith equal to sight. What does it say about blindness?

— What is Christ saying about himself when he refers to Shepherd and sheep? Look at Ezek 34, II Sam 7:8, Mic 5:1-3, Psalms 23,80 and 100.

MATERIAL AND DISCUSSION QUESTIONS FOR SESSION SIXTEEN

John 11

— The raising of Lazarus is always considered in a different category to the rest of the raising miracles (Mk 6:21ff, Lk 7:11ff) Spot the differences.

— This incident introduces the rest of the book; what important connections are there between this chapter and the story of the death of Jesus?

A Skirmish with Death
John 11

A first century apostle must have got some strange reactions to his gospel of Jesus: "What! Are you trying to tell me that this fellow Jesus who ended up strung up on a cross is the King the Jews we are waiting for? Some leader to be asking decent people to follow." "Jesus! He got the chop, didn't he? I heard he was some sort of revolutionary or carpenter king. Well, all I know is, the Roman system of law might have its faults, but it's basically a good one, and a just one. This town didn't know any peace until the Romans moved in. And if this Jesus of yours was put to death by the proper Roman authorities, he must have deserved it."

Christians who decorate rooms with crucifixes and begin their prayers by tracing a cross over themselves are bound to be a little insensitive to the scandal that the cross must have been in the Roman world. It was a shameful form of execution, a sign of weakness and humiliation, an obscene way to die. Jesus the Crucified was, in the eyes of the man in the street, the ultimate in failure.

Through Christian eyes, the picture is utterly transformed. What everyone else would think of as disaster, the Christian saw as the moment of triumph. Certainly, that triumph would have gone unnoticed if it were not for the Resurrection, but for writers like John, the real glory of Jesus is to be seen in his purest and most selfless act of love and obedience, his death. John especially is at pains to show that the Cross was no temporary triumph of the powers of darkness or setback for the mission of Christ. It is the culmination of all that Jesus came to do, an unequivocal statement of divine love in a loveless world. For this presentation, the second part of John's Gospel has earned the subtitle: the Book of Glory.

Many would see chapter eleven as closing the Book of Signs (see Session Twelve), but I would prefer to see it as opening the Book of Glory. Here we have in minature the conflict which Jesus will enter with death and his own triumph over it. Here, too, we see that his triumph is never meant to be his alone, but one in which all who believe in him will share. the scene leads very naturally into the beginning of the events of the final week, the royal anointing of chapter thirteen.

Our investigation of story in the last chapter should help us to see the drama and the meaning of this chapter. Perhaps this session might include a résumé on story and movement in story.

The movements of chapter eleven do not follow the patterns which we might expect. The first movement, which begins with the sickness of Lazarus, might have ended with Jesus coming to heal his friend. Certainly there are a few indications that this is what people thought that he would do. But it didn't happen. The next movement is that the death of a friend should bring mourning; and when Jesus went to Bethany and then to the tomb, this is what people thought that he came to do. But it wasn't (see the note on 11:33-37 below).

These frustrated movements help to underline the real movement involved in this chapter: death, linked with faith, can serve the purpose of giving glory to God, and this is seen through resurrection. True, Lazarus does not experience a real resurrection in a glorified body which will live forever. He is merely brought back to this life which he one day had to leave again. But his raising is a sign of Christ's ultimate victory over death which is to dominate the rest of the Fourth Gospel.

The light of Christ's final days is brought over the horizon by the fateful meeting of the High Priest's council. This meeting, which determines Jesus' fate, is occasioned by this very sign in Bethany. It also frames John's vision of the effects of Christ's saving death by an ironic interpretation of the words of Caiaphas. And from this chapter on, his impending death seems always present and prominent in the mind of Jesus.

There are two other areas which might be worthy of mention in connection with the story of the raising of Lazarus. One point is that raising Lazarus from the tomb is on a completely different plane for the first-century Jewish mentality than, say, the raising of the daughter of Jairus or of the widow's son in Nain; in the first three gospels, the people raised were dead, but not buried — that is, the full process of death was not complete. Also interesting to note in the Lazarus context is that the rabbis taught that after four days, there was absolutely nothing left of the life or identity of the deceased in the corpse.

In other words, while the raising of the dead in the miracles of the first three gospels is something wonderful, the raising of Lazarus is even more stupendous; the synoptics tell of how Jesus "cured" people who were no longer alive, but John 11 tells how he overcame the very grip of death. This outlook that death wasn't really final until burial is reflected in the ancient Creed: "...crucified, died and was buried."

The second area is sometimes called John's *realised eschatology*. The word eschatology might be a useful one for the members of the group to have, since they are bound to run across it if they read much on scriptural subjects elsewhere; it might be explained simply as the thinking which concerns the end of time (Greek *eschaton*, "the last thing"). While much of the eschatology of the New Testament seems to be expecting the Second Coming at any moment (although this can be an exaggerated impression), the Fourth Gospel does not seem to place the same importance on awaiting Christ's coming in glory. John's realised eschatology means that whatever the early Christians hope for at the end of time, the hopes for eternal life and resurrection especially, have already begun to be present with the coming of Jesus and enter each person's life when Christ is accepted by that person. This notion is present throughout John's Gospel, but comes to a climax in chapter eleven in the dialogue between Jesus and Martha (verses 23 to 27).

MATERIAL

John 11

AIM OF SESSION

To introduce the themes of the second part of John's gospel (the Book of Glory) through a reading of John 11.

The Book of Glory

In the first-century world, the cross was a symbol of shame and weakness and failure.

— so shameful that it was forbidden that a Roman citizen should die by crucifixion

— usually reserved for runaway slaves and insurrectionists

— must have been a huge obstacle in the preaching of Christ in a world that had respect for Roman law and order:

— implied that he had been some sort of criminal, if not revolutionary

— implied that he had been a failure

— Paul's reflection in 1 Cor 1:18,22-23

John has a unique treatment of the cross

— for him, it is the hour of Christ's glory

— it is the moment of the full revelation of what Jesus means and of who and what he is

— it is something which Christ approaches with the full freedom of love and obedience

— the second half of John's Gospel sometimes called "The Book of Glory"

Story and Chapter Eleven

The religious message of Scripture is often framed in story form; the structure of story is best approached in terms of its movement (see the notes for the last session.)

In chapter eleven, movement makes its impact because the story does not follow the lines that might be expected:

115

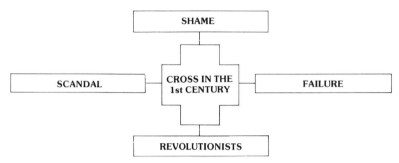

— the news that Lazarus is ill might be followed by a story of his healing, but it isn't (see verses 3 and 21)

— after the death, Jesus went down to Bethany; this could have been interpreted as wanting to go and mourn a friend (as is implied by verses 19 and 31 to 36), but this was not the purpose

The most unexpected movement in this chapter, that from death to the glory of God through resurrection, opens the main theme of the second part of John's Gospel.

11:1-5 The picture of Martha and Mary can be favourably compared with the picture in Luke 10:38ff., but in the Lucan passage there is no mention of Lazarus.

11:8 Jesus is outside of Judaea, and again the Judaean hostility is emphasised by the reaction of the disciples (as in 11:16).

11:9-10 An example of a parable in John, which can be interpreted along the following lines: Jesus, as light of the world, is in the world for a limited length of time (the twelve hours of the daylight); during this time, he cannot remain hidden, but must shine for the sake of humanity, despite the dangers.

11:21-24 Martha demonstrates a belief in the resurrection of the dead that she would hold in common with the Pharisees; but not all Jews would believe in the resurrection at the end of time (especially not the Saduccees). She also expresses a confidence in the authority of Jesus (11:22).

11:25 This *egō eimi* statement is the clearest example of John's so-called *realised eschatology*, that for John, Christian hope cannot tolerate the view that eternal life is something as remote as the end of time; as soon as a person believes in Jesus, eternal life has begun — as can be seen here and in many other passages in the gospel.

11:33-37 The emotion of Jesus in these verses seems on the surface to be that of a man mourning a friend, as the Judaeans interpret it. But the Judaeans usually *misinterpret* what Christ is at, and is it possible that Jesus mourns a friend whom he is about to raise from death? The Fourth Gospel might be speaking the language of miracles, workers and exorcists of the first century who, before attempting a mighty deed, would enter a state of deep emotion. Or perhaps this is John's "Agony in the Garden", where Christ is so deeply moved by the prospect of his own suffering and death at the tomb of his friend.

11:39 Jewish belief was that absolutely nothing remained of the life or identity of the deceased in a four day old corpse.

11:41-42 The prayer helps unlock the meaning of this raising miracle: it demonstrates that the Father hears and answers Jesus, and that it is he who has sent him. These are even more strongly demonstrated in the resurrection of Jesus himself.

11:45-46 The reaction is worthy of note: *many* of the Judaeans came to faith through this sign, but *some* went to the authorities and precipitated the final solution.

11:47-53 Caiaphas and his prophetic speech are prompted by this sign, and everything that follows in the gospel will bring Jesus quickly to the cross. The classic irony in the speech is that it could well be said by a political leader with an *eye* to expediency; he is saying that if the Romans see the following of Jesus as a messianic revolt, they might come and take away what little independence the Jews had left and destroy the Temple. The final solution was to get rid of Jesus so that the

nation could survive. For John, the meaning is quite different: belief in Christ would indeed lead to national extinction of a sort, because God would now be available to all nationalities and Israel's function as the lone people of God would be at an end. Whereas Caiaphas saw the death of Christ as bartering the life of one man for the life of a whole nation, John sees Christ giving his live in place of the life of all his people in his redeeming death. If anyone should ask the question, "Is it really possible that John knew the proceedings of the High Priest's Council?" refer the questioner to Jn 18:15.

QUESTIONS FOR DISCUSSION

— The raising of Lazarus is always considered in a different category to the rest of the raising miracles (Mk 6:21ff., Lk 7:11ff)
Spot the differences.

— This incident introduces the rest of the book; what important connections are there between this chapter and the story of the death of Jesus?

MATERIAL AND DISCUSSION QUESTIONS FOR SESSION SEVENTEEN

John 12

— In this chapter up to verse nineteen, how does John point out to the reader that Jesus is God's king? Why does John indicate this aspect of Christ at this point in the story?

— Verses 37 to 50 form a conclusion to the public ministry of Jesus in the Fourth Gospel; what do they have to say about accepting or rejecting Jesus?

The Kingly Messiah
John 12

John's Gospel draws the public ministry of Christ towards its end in this chapter, but to a certain extent it is already concluded. The last miraculous sign is recorded in chapter eleven, and even that sign is best seen as a rehearsal for the great drama of the final chapters of the gospel.

Chapter twelve opens the final week of the life of Jesus, and we can see the importance of the events of that final week by the overwhelming proportion of space given to it: the Fourth Gospel has a framework of a three-year ministry, and roughly eleven chapters of the gospel are concerned with those three years; but nine chapters deal with just one week. Mark's Gospel has the same type of proportion: ten chapters for the ministry, six chapters for the events of the final week. It isn't hard to see that this is the week that the evangelists felt was important to tell people about, and they do it in such a way that ensures that the reader knows the real meaning of these events.

The week begins with the anointing of Jesus' feet by Mary. There are many differences between this account and the passage in Mark 14:3-9, but the significance is the same: Jesus is anointed as King (and Messiah) before his death, for anointing was a sign of kingly (and priestly) inauguration. The anointing is explicitly put in the final week of the Fourth Gospel by the designation "six days before the Passover" and the drama is under way. The remark of Christ about his burial combines the messianic note with one of tragedy: his kingship will only be fulfilled by the Cross.

The triumphalism continues with the entry into Jerusalem. John refers to a passage in Zechariah (Zech 9:9), and many a Christian reader is content to leave it at that — another obscure Scripture has been fulfilled. Yet if we read on a bit in Zechariah, admittedly not one of the better known Old Testament books, we can see what type of a statement Jesus was making by riding a donkey. Horses were not very popular with the Scripture; in fact, at times the Old Testament seems to be definitely anti-horse. The reason is that in the ancient world the horse was a weapon of war, especially when connected to a chariot. If the king of Judah was building up his stables it was an ancient equivalent of stockpiling missiles, and for people like the prophets it demonstrated that the king's trust was in armaments, not in the Lord. The ideal king in Zech 9:9-10 is a king of peace, and that means that he must use an animal of peace for transport — there could be few animals of less use in a cavalry charge than the lowly ass. The contrast in modern terms would be something like the difference between a leader who rode in a parade in a tank and one who rode in parade on a push-bike. Even "humility" is too proud a word to describe it.

Yet it was a kingly entrance. The people shout "Hosanna", by this time a simply joyful acclamation, but in origin a word that means "Save us!" He is acclaimed "King of Israel", a public proclamation of his reign, and the lovely note in 12:16 that the disciples didn't have a clue as to what was going on at the time. That verse flashes like a neon sign to warn us to look deeply into all that follows, lest we be like the disciples and fail to comprehend.

A strange incident follows: "Greeks" (probably meaning Jews living in Greek territory) come up to Philip (who bears a Greek name) to arrange an audience with Jesus. It seems natural enough, but the reaction of Jesus is dramatic: if Greeks are looking for him, he is sufficiently in the spotlight to do his work, to give glory to the Father before all witnessing eyes.

Glory is such a central term in these final chapters that we might consider its levels of meaning. As a Greek word (*doxa*),

There could be few animals of less use in a cavalry charge than the lowly ass.

it started life meaning "opinion" and then drifted towards "good opinion" and finally ended up as meaning "fame, honour, glory". So John can talk about the Pharisees as people who wanted popularity, who prefer "the *doxa* of people to the *doxa* of God".

But glory is not just a Greek term, it is a Hebrew theological term as well. Its most important use was as a term to explain Yahweh's presence in the Temple. The normal Hebrew term for the Temple was simply "the House of Yahweh", probably reflecting a simplistic popular notion that God lived in the Temple. But the strong Old Testament teaching that Yahweh cannot be limited to a physical building (see 1 Kings 8:27, for instance) meant that the dwelling of Yahweh in the Temple needed qualification. The Old Testament answers the question "How does Yahweh live in the Temple?" in two ways: Yahweh's name is in the Temple (here people can call on his name, here Yahweh listens to prayer), and Yahweh's glory dwells in the Temple (here is where Yahweh is honoured and from here he shows his power).

This Old Testament use of "glory" is also lurking in the background of John's Gospel. As the glory of Yahweh filled the Temple at its consecration (1 Kgs 8:10-11), so Jesus is filled with the glory of the Father in his Passion. This ties in with John's portrayal of Jesus as the New Temple, the new place where God lives with his people, the new meeting place of God and humanity; the explicit identification of Jesus as the New Temple in the Fourth Gospel at the beginning of the ministry already connects this image with the Passion, Death and Resurrection (Jn 2:19-22). We will notice much use of the language of temple (such as "glory" and "name") and some temple imagery.

John, as we have noticed, delights in using more than one meaning of a word. We need only remember the "flowing/living" water ambiguity in chapter four or the "from above/again" ambiguity in chapter three. So too the Fourth Gospel here utilises both the ordinary meaning of glory as the good opinion of someone else and the theological meaning of Divine Presence among humanity in Jesus.

Jn 12:31-32 identifies two further meanings of the death of Christ. Firstly, it is a time of judgement for the prince of this world; even though it may appear a triumph, it will be his utter defeat. Secondly Christ's death is described by another dual-meaning word, *hupsoō*: the first level is that Christ will be "lifted up" on the cross, but the second meaning is that he will be "exalted" by this act, lifted up towards the heavenly realm to which he belongs, toward the Father whom he glorifes.

The last section (Jn 12:37-50) forms a concluding picture of the public ministry. It begins with a statement that people refused to believe despite the signs and continues with citations of Isaiah. The one in Jn 12:40 is problematic, but one approach is that the preaching of truth can harden the position of those opposed to the message. More interesting is the comment that Isaiah "saw Jesus' glory". The vision which is being referred to is undoubtedly the vision in Is 6:1-8, the vision of the presence of Yahweh in the Temple. More temple imagery! There is a bite in John's damning remark about people who prefer the good opinion of others to possession of the glory of God through faith in Jesus.

The discourse of Jn 12:44-50 summarises many of the themes of former discourses, highlighting the vital decision which each person must make concerning Jesus; the choice is between bringing judgement on oneself and being given eternal life. And with that strong statement of the importance of the decision facing all who hear the message of Jesus and his tremendous claims, the curtain closes on the ministry only to open on the climax in which Jesus completes his work as the Messiah and King sent by the Father.

MATERIAL

John 12

AIM OF SESSION

To begin John's account of the final week of Jesus, pointing out some of the themes which will recur in later chapters of the gospel.

SESSION NOTES

Jesus, the Kingly Messiah

— this chapter ends the public ministry and opens the eventful last week of Christ's life

— the last miraculous sign has already taken place in Jn 11

— John 11 also was a rehearsal of the struggle of life and death in tbe Book of Glory.

— the *Royal Anointing* of Jesus opens the final week

— the very title "Christ/Messiah" means "the anointed"

— there are differences between this and the account of Mk 14:3-9, although clearly the same incident is intended

12:1 The time note places this meal on the very first day of the final week, most likely the meal on Saturday night which marked the end of the Sabbath.

12:4-6 The introduction of Judas here (the statement is anonymous in Mark) reminds the reader of how near the betrayal is.

12:7 The kingly anointing is linked by Jesus with his death; the notion of Messiah is linked in all of the gospels with the necessity of suffering. In John, the kingship of Christ only gains prominence in the shadow of the cross.

The triumphant entry into Jerusalem continues the royal imagery of the anointing.

— the use of the donkey points to a king who is a man of peace, not using the military horse for a mount (see Zech 9:9-10)

— Jesus receives the acclamation of his kingship from the people in 12:13

12:12 Passover, being a pilgrimage feast, would have filled Jerusalem with visitors from all over the Roman world.

12:16 One of the reminders that not even the disciples understood what was happening, that it took the Resurrection to bring the significance of these events to light. It is also a warning to the reader to look beneath the surface at what is happening in this final week, lest a superficial approach miss the truth of the Cross.

The Hour of Glory

Jews from the Greek world, in Jerusalem for Passover, seek an audience with Jesus; this indication that he is so much in the spotlight that Jews from outside Palestine want to see him is a signal for Jesus that the time for his great work has arrived.

The term "glory" which peppers the last half of John's Gospel is another word with two distinct meanings, both of which John uses:

— the ordinary Greek meaning, "good opinion, fame"

— a term the Old Testament uses to descibe the way in which Yahweh lived in the Temple, his "glory" or his "name" lived there with his people in the building which could not contain Yahweh himself

— the second use is part of John's image of Jesus as the New Temple, the new meeting place of God and humanity, the place where God is given perfect worship (cf. Jn 2:19-22)

12:20-22 These Greek Jews (not Greek pagans) approach Philip (who bears a Greek name). Jesus does not seem to grant them the interview, but sees the request as a signal that he is enough in the spotlight for his great act of "giving glory" to the Father.

12:24 The fruitful grain of wheat is also used in the parable of Mk 4:1-9 and, more relevant to the Johannine use, in 1 Cor 15:36-38 to describe the wonder of resurrection life. The message is clear: death might seem to lead to extinction, but for Jesus it will lead to abundant fruitfulness.

12:27 The Fourth Gospel shows that obedience was not an easy decision for Jesus to make although he embraced obedience fully.

12:31-33 The glorification means the defeat of the "Prince of this world", although it may seem to be his victory. The word Jesus uses to describe his death has two meanings: "to be lifted up" which describes the physical act of crucifixion, and "to be exalted" which describes the theological reality.

Conclusion of the Public Ministry

The Fourth Gospel ends the public ministry with concluding comments on the reaction which Jesus has received and then a discourse which re-emphasises the important choice facing all who hear of Christ.

12:37-40 The refusal of many to believe is set against the insights of Isaiah. One approach to what Isaiah is saying is that the proclaiming of God's message can have the effect of hardening the position of its opponents rather than of converting them.

12:41 The mention of Isaiah seeing Christ's glory probably refers to the Temple vision of Isaiah chapter six, reinforcing John's picture of Jesus as the New Temple.

12:42-43 Rejection is an act of free will; the rejectors prefer the good opinion of others to the good opinion of God and his dwelling among them in Jesus.

12:44-50 This discourse combines themes from the earlier discourses as a last statement on the necessity to choose Jesus; themes such as: the One who sent Jesus, Christ as light of the world, condemnation and judgement contrasted with the saving purpose of Christ's mission, and the faithful fulfilling of what the Father sent Jesus to do.

QUESTIONS FOR DISCUSSION

— On this chapter up to verse nineteen, how does John point out to the reader that Jesus is God's king? Why does John indicate this aspect of Christ at this point in the story?

— Verses 37 to 50 form a conclusion to the public ministry of Jesus in the Fourth Gospel; what do they have to say about accepting or rejecting Jesus?

DISCUSSION QUESTIONS FOR
SESSION EIGHTEEN

John 13-14

— Compare the first part of this chapter with Lk 22:24-30 (and take note of the setting) and Phil 2:5-11. What aspect of Christ's ministry is being highlighted? What does this say about the death of Christ?

— According to chapter fourteen, what benefit will the death of Christ be for the disciples?

The Last Supper Begins

John 12-14

The one incident which most Christians associate with the Last Supper is missing from John's account of that night, and yet he doesn't skimp on space. In fact, about a fourth of the gospel is put into this scenario (chapters thirteen to seventeen), most of it in the form of a long set of discourses to the apostles. There is a certain biblical tradition of the last words of great figures: Jacob blessing his twelve sons (and thus the twelve tribes descended from them) on his deathbed in Gen 49:1-27, Moses giving his last instructions in the Book of Deuteronomy, and David's rather unedifying deathbed speech in 1 Kings 2:2-9. So the Last Supper discourses fit an Old Testament model, that the great figures of history often make important speeches before their death. But there is also a model within the Fourth Gospel itself, in the Book of Signs: there the signs are followed by a discourse which brings out the meaning of the sign. So what is the sign which these five chapters elucidate? Here is the twist: instead of a sign followed by a discourse, in these chapters the discourse comes before the sign. The order of items in scriptural writing is like a liturgical procession: the more important comes after the less important. In the Book of Signs, the sign itself was always treated as less important than the disclosure of its meaning. The feeding of the multitude, for instance, is not nearly as important as the consideration of Jesus as Bread of Life, or the opening of a blind man's eyes takes second place to a blind man seeing who Jesus really is. On that principle alone, the order here must be reversed, for the sign is the Cross and Resurrection, and the explanation of those events is far inferior to the happenings themselves.

In a way, the institution narratives of the other three gospels serve the same purpose. When Jesus refers to broken bread as his body and speaks of his blood poured out for many, he is not just instituting a sacrament but showing the meaning of his death. In the sacramental signs his death is displayed as a self-giving for humanity and the basis of a new covenant with God. John brings out the richness of the death and resurrection by a discourse instead.

Another item which will not escape the careful reader (and blessed are you if you have noticed this without anyone to point it out!) is the seam of Jn 14:31 which ties with Jn 18:1. Put together, they read like this:

> "But let the world know that I love the Father and just as he commanded me, so do I do. Get up, let's go from here". Having said these things, Jesus left with his disciples across the Kedron Valley where there was a garden into which he and his disciples entered.

The problem is that between the suggestion that the group move on and the narrator's note that they moved came three chapters of discourse! This should be enough to make us suspect that the Fourth Gospel as we have it is not a first draft, but that it has gone through at least one revision. For those who are interested in such questions, there are other bits of evidence to buttress such a theory. Among them:

1) John's Gospel comes to a very neat conclusion in Jn 20:30-31, ending on an up-beat stroke of faith without seeing. But the gospel goes on for another chapter; someone has added an epilogue. And one of the concerns of this chapter is that there is a rumour that the beloved disciple would never die; it seems that someone discounts the validity of the rumour, probably because the disciple has in fact died.

2) The ending of that epilogue is an echo of the conclusion at the end of Jn 20, but with a strange passing remark: "This is the disciple who witnesses about these things, and who wrote them, and *we know* that his witness is true" (Jn 21:24). This reads like an endorsement from someone other than the beloved disciple and quite probably points to those who produced and promulgated the later edition.

3) The existence of blocks of material which do not run smoothly with the general outline of the gospel might be an indication of inclusions by the later editors of incident and discourse which wasn't part of the first edition. This note in Jn 14:31 shows that Jn 15-17 is one such block. Perhaps Jn 9 is another. It should be added quickly that these portions

do fit the Johannine way of thinking and speaking; in other words, the later editors seem to have worked with other Johannine material of which they were aware which wasn't already included in the first edition.

4) The last indication which I will mention is one of the strongest and most obvious. It is well known even to Christians who rarely open the Scriptures that the Fourth Gospel never calls John by name and that a usual term for him is "the disciple whom Jesus loved". This anonymity is usually recognised for what it is, an act of great humility, a statement that "I'm not the important one in this story; Jesus is." But what type of humility is it to go around under the label, "beloved disciple"? In fact, there are places where this anonymous figure is simply called "another disciple" (as in Jn 18:15) or just one of two (as in Jn 1:35-40). Could "the disciple whom Jesus loved" be evidence of a bit of editing, those who valued this anonymous figure not allowing him to be given less than his true standing in the narrative?

As much as questions of authorship may intrigue the Hercule Poirot in all of us, they are not as important as what is being said in the book. We'll return to this first section of the Last Supper in John to examine some of its perspectives on the events of the next few days.

The first pointer to the meaning of the Cross and Resurrection is an action of Jesus, the washing of his disciples' feet. It is obviously an image of service and self-giving. There is also the characteristic mystery about Jesus as he sets about the task; without a single word of explanation, he moves from head of the group to the work of the servant. No wonder Peter objected! Yet even in the face of the objection, Christ does not explain what he is at until the whole action is complete. Another overtone lurks behind this scene, however; its presence is betrayed by Jn 13:8, "Jesus answered him, 'If I do not wash you, you have no part with me'." John might well be using the washing image to conjure up ideas of Baptism. The practice of the early Church would seem to endorse such a view, since Baptism was given as the first item in a celebration of the Eucharist (after the Church had settled down a bit after its initial missionary thrust). Then, too, the notion of being baptised into the death and resurrection of Christ might be behind the answer to Peter's objection: if he is not washed, Peter will have no share in the coming events. The explicit emphasis, however, is the service which the disciples are to render each other after the pattern of Christ's service, a service which is to be seen in its fullness the following day.

The Fourth Gospel, along with the other three, places a special importance on the fact that Jesus knows exactly what is about to take place. Our doctrinal outlook accepts this naturally as an aspect of Christ's divine foreknowledge, but that is not the impact of this foreknowledge in the gospels. The evangelists are telling us that Jesus is not taken by surprise nor frustrated and foiled by the Cross; it is all part of the plan of action, and he is fully in control of the course of events. This is bought out in Jn 13:19, "From the start I tell you this before it happens, so that you may believe when it happens that *ego eimi*." These events are not tragedy nor disgrace, but the glorification of the Son and the Father (cf. Jn 13:31-32 and the discussion of *glory* in Session Seventeen).

The New Commandment of Jn 13:34-35 is identified by

many Christians as the familiar second Great Commandment (cf. Lk 10:25-29), but there are differences. The second Great Commandment was to love one's neighbour as oneself, and the parable of the good Samaritan extended neighbour to include everyone that you come into contact with, even your enemy. This commandment is not about everyone, but about loving "one another", that is, about the love between Christians. Even the degree of love is changed, raised above even the intensity of self-love to "just as much as I loved you".

It is not termed a "New" Commandment simply to draw our attention to the differences between this commandment and those that have gone before. A New Commandment draws attention to a New Covenant. The pattern is already set in the Old Testament: when a covenant was made with Noah, the commandments about respecting life and subduing the earth were given (Gen 9:1-9); the covenant with Abraham brought the commandment of circumcision (Gen 17:1-10); the covenant with Moses is entwined with the Old Testament Law (Ex 20-24). So the New Covenant established by the death of Jesus brings its own New Commandment.

Chapter fourteen contains much teaching on the meaning of Christ's death, bringing out that, even though it be sad, it is necessary (14:27-31). It makes possible the dwelling of the disciples with God, just as in Jesus divinity has made its home for so long with man (14:1-6). Once more it is stressed that the Father is clearly seen in the activity and the person of Jesus; he is our knowledge of the Father and the Father's Word to us (Jn 14:8-11). The work of Jesus continues in the disciples (14:12-14), especially through the abiding presence of the Spirit who dwells with them (14:16-17). Those who keep Christ's commands will always know Jesus, even after his departure, for his home is with them (Jn 14:21-24), and the Spirit will bring them full understanding (14:26).

These chapters, as we have seen, probably constitute a full treatment of the Last Supper in their own right. But they do not exhaust the perspective of the Fourth Gospel (as we have it) on that great night, and many of the ideas first presented in Jn 13-14 will be more fully developed in the next few chapters.

MATERIAL

John 13-14

AIM OF SESSION

To introduce the insights of Jn 13-14 into the mystery of Christ's death and resurrection; to show some of the reasons for saying that John's Gospel as we have it shows the work of a later editor.

SESSION NOTES

The Last Supper in the Fourth Gospel

— Holy Thursday night occupies a disproportionate amount of space in the Fourth Gospel

— chapters thirteen to seventeen are concerned solely with the Last Supper

— this follows a biblical pattern for the important last speeches of great figures, such as Jacob and Moses

— it also follows John's practice of connecting sign and discourse

— usually the discourse follows the sign, emphasising that the discourse is more central

— here the sign follows the discourse, since the sign (the Death and Resurrection) is the climax of the whole gospel story

— there is no account in John of the institution of the Eucharist

— there is no lack of eucharistic language in the Fourth Gospel (e.g. Jn 6)

— one reason could be that John's Gospel, aimed at both believers and interested non-believers, was written at the time when the liturgical rites were not revealed to anyone except the baptised

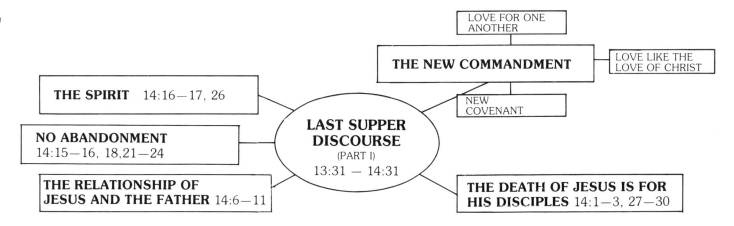

— as is the case with the institution narratives, John's account of the Last Supper brings out the deeper meaning of the events which are about to happen

Jn 14:31, especially when read with Jn 18:1, indicates that the Fourth Gospel as we have it has undergone at least a second edition.

— the epilogue of chapter twenty-one after the conclusion at the end of chapter twenty

— the affirmation at the end of the epilogue that "we know" the witness behind the gospel is reliable

— blocks of material which do not quite fit into the structure of the gospel (as in the case of the material following 14:31)

— the substitution of "disciple whom Jesus loved" for the more anonymous "other disciple"

— the conclusion would be that the original draft of the gospel was expanded to include other Johannine material by a follower or followers of the disciple after his death

The Washing of the Feet of the Disciples

The first insight into the meaning of the Cross is in an action of service which Jesus makes for his disciples.

There might be an overtone of Baptism here, especially in the dialogue between Christ and Peter (13:6-8).

Of prime importance is the example of service which Jesus sets for his followers.

13:1 John shows that he is now beginning the narrative of a great drama, one which is characterised by the love of Jesus. Verse two shows that it is a cosmic drama, not a merely human one: Satan is acting through the opponents of Christ, especially through his betrayer.

13:4 The wordlessness of Christ should be noted. First comes the sign, and then its meaning. It also brings out that the disciples found it difficult to understand what Jesus said and did; indeed, they failed until after the Resurrection.

13:10-11 The foreknowledge of Christ concerning his betrayal highlights his complete control over the events of these days, and his freedom in going to his death. This foreknowledge is also present in 13:19.

13:12-17 The washing of feet was an example of service, and the lesson of service at the Last Supper is also present in Lk 22:24-30. It is also a demonstration of the service which Jesus is about to give to his followers by his death, and so the discourse on service flows naturally into talk of his betrayal (13:18-30).

The New Commandment

The love command in John's Gospel is clearly called "new". Christian ears can mishear this in two different ways:

— it is new because no one ever commanded love before (grossly mistaken);

— it is not new because Jesus already gave the Two Great Commandments which are both love commands.

The love command here is, in fact, different from the Second Great Commandment ("Love thy neighbour as thyself") in two ways:

— this love command concerns "one another", that is, other Christians, whereas "thy neighbour" includes all of humanity (Lk 10:25-37);

— this command goes beyond "as thyself" all the way to "as I have loved you".

The giving of a new commandment meant the making of a New Covenant

— the Fourth Gospel links the Last Supper as a meal of the New Covenant in this way; the other three do the same thing by giving an account of the institution of the Eucharist

— the giving of a new commandment at the time the making of a covenant can be observed in Gen 9:1-9, Gen 17:1-10 and Ex 19-24

The Greek word which the New Testament uses of love (*agapē*) is more precise than our word in English:

— it has no emotional overtones of affection like other Greek words for love; Christian love does not depend on liking a person

— it is a very practical sort of love, one that gets things done rather than just remaining a warm feeling about someone; it is quite close to English words like "care" or "concern"

13:31-32 The theme of glory is repeated. The Passion will be the glory both of the Son and of the Father. It will also be the time when Christ, the new Temple, is consecrated and filled with the glory of the Father to become the unique meeting place of God and humanity and the place where perfect sacrifice is offered to the Father.

13:35 The Jews living among the pagans were known because of their life-style, a direct result of their observance of the covenant commandments. Practices such as the non-eating of certain foods, the Sabbath observance, even circumcision, made them distinguishable throughout the known world. Now Jesus wants those who live by his covenant to also be noticeable because of their observance of his commandment, the love that they have for one another.

The Departure of Jesus

Chapter fourteen takes the problem of the departure by Jesus from his disciples; if we take Jn 14:31 as ending the Last Supper discourse in the "first edition", then this chapter constitutes a Farewell discourse in its own right.

127

Among the ideas which are brought out in this context are these:

— that the death of Jesus is to the advantage of his disciples (14:1-3, 27-30)

— the relationship of Jesus and the Father (14:6-11)

— that those who obey the commandment of Jesus will not be abandoned (14:15-16,18,21-24)

— the Spirit who is with the disciples (14:16-17,26)

14:7-11 The heart of Trinitarian theology: what we *see* in Jesus is also in the Father (and in the Spirit); three distinct persons does not mean three distinct personalities. Those who think of Jesus as kind and gentle in contrast to a Father who is angry and merciless would be hard pressed to justify their theories in the gospels!

14:12-14 I Kings 8:29-53, Solomon prays that every prayer offered in the newly built Temple be heard. Now it is not in a building in Jerusalem where prayers will be heard, but in the name of Jesus, so that the glory of the Father will be seen in the Son.

14:16 *Paraclētos* is a word that can mean adviser or defence lawyer or helper; it is here used about the Spirit but in 1 Jn 2:1 it is used to describe Jesus himself.

14:26 This is a verse used to establish the "personhood" of the Spirit. In Greek the word for Spirit (*pneuma*) is neuter and usually takes neuter pronouns and adjectives; but there, the masculine pronoun is used, which demonstrates that the Spirit is not an impersonal "it", but a person acting in the scheme of salvation, just like Jesus or the Father.

14:30-31 The "Prince of this world" is let have his way, not because he has the power to force his will on Christ, but so that in his death Jesus can demonstrate his love of the Father, and that in his resurrection, the Father can affirm that Jesus has indeed acted as the Father commanded.

QUESTIONS FOR DISCUSSION

— Compare the first part of this chapter with Lk 22:24-30 (and take note of the setting) and Phil 2:5-11. What aspect of Christ's ministry is being highlighted?

— What does this say about the death of Christ?

— According to chapter fourteen, what benefit will the death of Christ be for the disciples?

MATERIAL AND DISCUSSION QUESTIONS FOR SESSION NINETEEN

John 15-16

— In the light of Ps 80 and Is 5:1-7, should Jn 15:1-8 be applied to the individual relationship with Christ, or to the whole Church?

— What is the work of the Spirit according to chapter sixteen?

Last Supper Insights

All of the gospels, but most especially Matthew's, are great for finding hints about Christ's coming in the Old Testament. We are so used to this sort of thing that we nearly think that the real purpose of the Old Testament (or the prophets, at any rate) was to drop such hints about the coming Messiah. Over the centuries, that outlook was so developed that it almost become a theological discipline in its own right, a study we call "typology", wherein everything in the Old Testament was seen as a type (or example or foreshadowing) of some Christian reality. Of course, the thing went to extremes: Solomon's wives were once seen as his virtues and his concubines as representing his vices; Solomon ruled successfully, according to this school of thought, because his virtues (his seven hundred wives) outnumbered his vices (his three hundred concubines). Typology, let it be stressed, is not in vogue today.

The Fourth Gospel has its own special type of typology, however. It sees dim mirrors of the reality of Jesus in nature: the light which gives direction and knowledge is a type for the real guidance that comes with Christ; the relationship of trust and protection between sheep and shepherd speaks of Christ and his people; the life-giving nourishment of bread is representative of the life-giving nourishment which humanity can find in Christ; even the door to the sheepfold is a sign for the one through whom one must enter to be among God's people. And Christ applies all of these realities to himself, often using the special *egō eimi* phrase: "I am the light of the world", "I am the good shepherd", "I am the bread of life", "I am the door to the sheepfold." And there are other things in the world around us which Jesus says point to what he is and does and brings: refreshing water, the free-blowing wind, the grain that can only be fruitful if it dies. It is as if the whole of creation is hinting at something, but the hints are feeble and fragile; only reality is real, and the reality is Christ.

One of the strongest of these Johannine "nature hints" opens the second section of the Last Supper. In this section, some of the ideas of the first section are repeated: the Spirit, prayer in the name of Jesus, the relationship to the Father, the departure of Christ (see the last Session). The image of the vine is new, however, and is an image with more than one level of meaning.

The vine is recalled for its unity, something which can be seen by anyone who looks at a vine. Christ describes himself as the vine and his disciples as the branches, yet, when looking at a vine, who can say where the vine ends and the branches begin? This idea of each Christian being part of a larger reality, and the larger reality being Jesus, seems very much like a Johannine restatement of Paul's description of the Church as the Body of Christ (cf. 1 Cor 12:12-27). Also on this level of physical nature itself are introduced images of fruitfulness and pruning.

The next level of meaning is found in the use the Old Testament makes of vine imagery. Psalm 80 describes Israel as the vine which Yahweh has planted; chapter fifteen of Ezekiel uses a vine image for the people left in Jerusalem with rather less complimentary applications. The fifth chapter of Isaiah contains a song about the trouble that a man can go to for his vineyard, only to be disappointed in its fruits; Isaiah applies the song to Israel and Yahweh: At this level, the talk of a vine conjures up the people of Israel, a people that Yahweh has planted, a people Yahweh meant to be fruitful.

Who can say where the vine ends and the branch begins.

The last level of meaning comes from Christ's use of the image in this chapter, demonstrating what the "types" were all about. The unity of a vine and its branches is a type for the unity of Jesus and his followers. Its fruitfulness and pruning are reminders that each branch must give proof that it is alive and worth its space. Even the people of Israel become a type for the Church; by their election and productivity they were meant to show signs of the election and fruitfulness of the new people of God. But Isaiah and Ezekiel make them a negative sign; they become a warning to Christians to produce the expected fruits.

The work of the Spirit is also expounded in this second part of the Last Supper discourses, but more fully than in the first part. Jn 16:8-11 uses a verb which means to convict or expose so that we could translate it: "And when he comes he will show the world to be wrong about sin and about righteousness and about judgement." To paraphrase the following verses, the world is wrong about sin because they did not believe in Jesus (and that non-belief after all that he had said and done is the greatest triumph of sin); the world is wrong about righteousness since the one whom it condemned was in fact received by the Father; the world is wrong about judgement since its ruler, the one who leads the world's rebellion against God, stands condemned. These verses summarise the deep divide that the Fourth Gospel sees between those who accept Jesus and those who reject him. In typically Jewish fashion, the world of belief and non-belief is painted in what are today the unfashionable hues of black and white.

Often the apostles in John's Gospel — along with everyone else — misunderstand what Jesus says and does. The Spirit is the guarantee that this great misunderstanding is not continuing among his disciples and that the gospel we read is an authentic interpretation of his words and deeds. In the promises of the Spirit at the Last Supper, we are told that the Spirit, who is the Spirit of Truth, will "make a way into all the truth" for us. His message is the same as the message of Jesus, only with his speaking of it will come proper understanding. That will bring glory to the Son in turn (Jn 16:12-15). The description of the Spirit as one who leads the Church to truth is reminiscent of the words Vatican II uses to speak of the role of tradition in the life of the Church:

> The tradition that comes from the apostles makes progress in the Church, with the help of the Holy Spirit. There is a growth in insight into the realities and words that are being passed on. This comes about in various ways. It comes through the contemplation and study of believers who ponder these things in their hearts. It comes from the intimate sense of spiritual realities which they experience. And it comes from the preaching of those who have received, along with their right of succession in the episcopate, the sure charism of truth. Thus, as the centuries go by, the Church is always advancing towards the plentitude of divine truth, until eventually the words of God are fulfilled in her. (Vatican II, *Dei Verbum*, para. 8.)

The ending of this section also brings out a theme developed elsewhere in the gospel: those who do not understand the origins of Jesus also fail to accept his message. In Jn 16:25-33, Jesus "speaks plainly" about his origin and his destiny; the profession of faith by the disciples (16:29-30) reflects the centrality of this revelation. But their faith is still questionable, since they will abandon Christ during his hour of glorification (16:31-32).

MATERIAL

John 15-16

AIM OF SESSION

To investigate the use of nature imagery in the Fourth Gospel; to continue the Last Supper discourses in the Fourth Gospel.

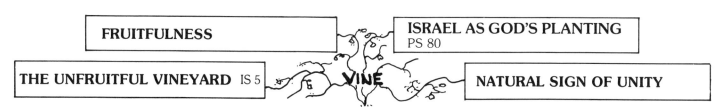

| FRUITFULNESS | ISRAEL AS GOD'S PLANTING
PS 80 |

| THE UNFRUITFUL VINEYARD IS 5 | VINE | NATURAL SIGN OF UNITY |

SESSION NOTES

Jesus, the True Vine

Much of the New Testament sees in Jesus the "fulfilment" of the Old Testament; that is, the Old Testament presents ideas and images which are clarified in the person of Christ.

— often this "fulfilment" is over and above the plain meaning of the Old Testament passage itself, and for this reason is sometimes called the *sensus plenior* or "fuller sense"

— sometimes this was an Old Testament figure or story which is echoed in the figure and story of Jesus — such as Moses who received the Law on Mount Sinai who is alluded to in the first gospel's picture of Jesus giving a New Law in the Sermon on the Mount (Mt 5-7); in this case, the Old Testament figure or incident is seen as a *type* or foreshadowing of what would come with Christ

John's Gospel sees in nature hints and insights into the meaning of Jesus, and often applies these in the *ego eimi* statements.

— the nourishment of bread is a pointer to the essential nourishment of Jesus to the one who feeds on him: I am the bread of life

— the guiding, illuminating brightness of the sun is a pointer to the sight Jesus is to those who follow him: I am the light of the world

— the attachment between sheep and shepherd, the protective concern of the shepherd and the trust of the sheep is a pointer to the relationship between Jesus and the people he has made his own: I am the good shepherd

Even these nature images have levels of association from the Old Testament and the religious life of the first century Jews. (Session Fifteen gives some of the Old Testament background to the shepherd image, for example.)

In the Last Supper section of the Fourth Gospel, the nature image which is evoked is that of the vine.

— at the level of pure nature, the vine is used as a symbol of unity and fruitbearing

— the Old Testament uses vine as a symbol of Israel, God's own planting (Ps 80); it is also used as an image of unfruitful gardening as Israel has disappointed Yahweh (Is 5)

— the vine image would have had particular relevance to the Last Supper where Christ had blessed God for giving "the fruit of the vine"; it may be viewed as a eucharistic image

15:4 The Christian only bears fruit insofar as he or she "remains" in Christ. The notion of remaining might be considered an aspect of what Paul calls *pistis*, faithfulness or faith.

15:5 The unity of branch and vine is similar to Paul's unity of member with the Body. Every use of "you" in this passage is plural, for John is not speaking of some mystical union of the individual with Christ, but the unity of all disciples in Jesus.

15:9-12 "Remaining" is linked to the commandment of love for one another.

15:13-17 The love commandment is clarified by the highest example of love, the death of Jesus which is about to take place. The love of Jesus for his disciples is also displayed by the message which he has given them, the full revelation of the Father; it can also be seen in his choice of them and in their bearing fruit.

15:18-25 The disciples, who as branches of the True Vine are his presence in the world, will receive the same kind of rejection as Christ did. Popularity and respectability should make Christians do a bit of soul-searching more than apparent failure to be acceptable to everyone.

The Coming Paraclete

— one significance of the departure of Jesus from his disciples is that the Spirit will come to them

— the major role of the Spirit might be seen under the umbrella of "witness":

— he will bear witness that the world was wrong and that Jesus was right (Jn 16:8-11)

— he will witness by bringing understanding of the meaning of Jesus' words and actions to the apostles (Jn 16:12-15)

15:26 The Paraclete is designated the "Spirit of Truth". Certainly John intends that title to focus on his function of bringing witness to the truth to the disciples; but John, in his characteristic twin meanings for one term, might intend to speak of the Spirit as the Spirit of the Covenant which Jesus seals (truth standing for *'emeth*, covenant loyalty and steadfastness).

16:1-4 The foreknowledge of Jesus is again displayed to show that he is in control of the events which follow (see Session Eighteen).

16:8-11 The world (the human systems that cannot accept Jesus) is wrong about sin and righteousness and judgement, for it does not see that real sin is the rejection of Jesus, that real righteousness is to be found in the one it has condemned and yet the Father accepts, and that condemnation really applies to the "ruler of this world".

16:12-15 The disciples move from incomprehension to true understanding only after the Resurrection, that is, after the Spirit has been given to them. Compare Luke's approach in Acts of the Apostles: before the descent of the Spirit, the disciples throw lots to discover God's will (Acts 1:26); but after the Spirit is with them, *they* make decisions in his name (Acts 15:28).

16:20-22 The grief of the death of Christ is fruitful, like a mother's labour pain, for it heralds the coming of a new reality: the Resurrection of Jesus (and the coming of the Spirit).

Speaking Plainly

Confusion permeates John's Gospel, indicating that the words and deeds of Jesus were not fully understood by those who heard and saw him; on the part of the multitude, much of this confusion is expressed by statements which show that the crowds do not understand the origin of Jesus:

— they think that they know where he comes from (7:27-28)

— they call him a Samaritan (8:48)

— they say that he cannot be from God (9:16)

— they admit that they do not know where he comes from (9:29)

The only accurate way to describe the origins of Jesus is from above (*anōthen*), from God (3:31-36); were people to understand this, they would perceive the real meaning of Christ.

— the cross would lift Christ back to the realm of the above from which he comes (3:11-14)

— this lifting up will draw humanity to Jesus (12:32-33)

The final statement in the Last Supper discourses is a plain statement of Jesus' origin and his destiny; it evokes an acclamation of perception from the apostles which Jesus says is still deficient.

16:25-28 The heart of this statement can be found in verse twenty-eight; there Jesus says plainly that he has come from the Father and he is going to the Father.

16:29-30 The affirmation by the disciples picks up the central revelation: now that they know that Jesus comes from God, they think that they have their understanding (and thus their faith) perfected. Christ points to how they will react in his hour as the proof that they still have some way to go.

QUESTIONS FOR DISCUSSION

— In the light of Psalm 80 and Is 5:1-7, should Jn 15:1-8 be applied to the individual relationship with Christ, or to the whole Church?

— What is the work of the Spirit accoridng to chapter sixteen?

MATERIAL AND DISCUSSION QUESTIONS FOR SESSION TWENTY

John 17
— This chapter has been styled the priestly prayer of Christ for his Church; what does Christ ask for his Church?

— How is the body of disciples linked to the intimate relationship of Jesus and the Father?

The Priestly Prayer
John 17

The seventeenth chapter of John is one of those sections of the gospels which is very familiar to most Christians; quite apart from its poetic qualities, its use for prayers and meditations on Christian unity has driven its wording deep into our awareness. The disadvantage is that the main (if not only) feature of the passage which is noticed by many on a first reading is the one which they expect to find: the theme of unity.

There are other striking aspects of this passage, however, which should be brought to the attention of the group. In the structure of the Fourth Gospel, chapter seventeen represents the last extended discourse of Jesus in the presence of his disciples; so if there is a certain importance on the last words of a biblical figure which lay behind the whole of the Last Supper discourses, this importance is even more to be seen in this passage.

There is another element, nearly a "human interest" element. The synoptic tradition, and especially Luke's Gospel, shows Jesus spending great amounts of time in prayer. Yet there is not a lot of information as to the type of prayer which he was engaged in. Here we have an example of what Jesus prayed for, an insight into what went on during those long nights spent in prayer. Even if we do not possess the exact words and phrases of Jesus in these verses — or even elsewhere in the Fourth Gospel — we do have sentiments which are authentic, and it is those sentiments which matter.

In the context of the Fourth Gospel, it is noteworthy that this prayer comes in the context of "plain speaking" (Jn 16:29). The disciples are allowed to overhear the intimate conversation of Jesus with his Father. The mystery of the Cross and its meaning are also spoken of: Christ's death occurs in the hour of glorification (17:1); it happens so that he may give eternal life to believers (17:2); through the cross and resurrection, the Father will give glory to the Son (17:5); Christ's death brings Christ back to the Father (17:11). The prayer is intimately woven with the events which are about to take place.

Familiar themes resound throughout this prayer. Glory and Name come together in this prayer, terms which — as we have already seen (Session Seventeen) — have strong connotations of God's presence with his people in the Temple. They are also terms used in the Jewish tradition of prayers of praise and thanksgiving. Even today, the response to the first sentence of Israel's daily prayer, the *shema*, is "Blessed is the Name of the Glory of his Kingdom forever and ever". The relationship between Jesus and the Father also occupies a key position in this chapter; the mission of Jesus and the unity between himself and his Father reach their climax here, and are extended to include the disciples. As Jesus was sent by the Father, the disciples are about to be sent into the world; so Jesus prays for their consecration so that they can make Jesus and the Father known. Their unity will confirm that Jesus was sent by the Father; their unity is not simply among themselves, but rooted in their unity with the Father and the Son. A natural climax is reached for the set of discourses which began on service of the love for one another.

One last consideration on the chapter is cautiously proposed: did the eucharistic practice of the early Church have an influence on the framing of chapter seventeen? It is a difficult question to answer, since the evidence which we have of the very early Eucharistic Prayers is scanty, to say the least. The Christians of the first few centuries had a horror of speaking directly about the sacraments to the non-baptised (something which might be an influence behind John's omission of the institution of the Eucharist). The earliest Eucharistic prayer that we possess seems to be from a probably second-century source, the *Didachē*. Leaving aside the rubrics, it reads:

> We give you thanks, our Father,
> for the holy vine of David your son,
> which you revealed to us through your son Jesus.
>
> We give you thanks, our Father,
> for the life and revelation
> which you have revealed to us through your son Jesus.
> To you be glory forever.
> Just as this broken bread was scattered
>   on the mountains,

just as it was gathered and made into One,
so may your Church be gathered
from the earth's boundaries
into the Kingdom together.
For yours are the glory and the power through
    Jesus Christ forever.

We give you thanks, Holy Father, for your holy Name,
which you have made to dwell in our hearts,
and for the revelation and faith and life without end
which you have revealed through your son Jesus.
To you be glory forever.
You yourself, all-powerful ruler,
did create everything for your Name's sake,
giving food and drink for human enjoyment
so that they should thank you.
But us you have blessed with spiritual food and drink
and life forever through your son.
For everything we thank you since you are mighty.
To you be glory forever.
Remember, Lord, your Church:
deliver her from every evil and bring her to the
    fullness of love.
And gather her together from the four winds,
    make her holy,
and bring her into your Kingdom, which you have
    prepared for her.
For yours are the power and glory forever.
Let grace come and this world pass away.
Hosanna to the God of David.
If any be holy, let him come; if any be not,
    let him reform.
Maranatha. Amen.

Perhaps on first sight this prayer from the *Didachē* does not seem to bear much resemblance to either the Eucharistic Prayer as we know it or to the seventeenth chapter of John.

Indeed, the prayer was not said as a unit (as our Eucharistic Prayers are), but was divided into sections before and after the distribution. Some liturgists have hesitation in calling the prayer a Eucharistic Prayer, although most would agree that this was its original context. In using it to approach chapter seventeen, we are reminded that the early Eucharistic Prayers could be very different from the structure which we accept as normal.

It is not the structure which is similar to John 17, however, as much as the ideas. In the prayer from the *Didachē* there are many references to glory, name, unity and revelation from the Father — all themes which play their part in the Fourth Gospel's prayer. Another ancient prayer which is in the context of the Eucharist — though not from as reputable a source — is to be found in the second century apocryphal Acts of John. That prayer too is full of familiar terms from John 17: glory, name, only God, world. The evidence from outside the New Testament itself would at least raise the possibility that John 17 was related to the type of prayer which would be made at the early celebration of the Eucharist. The suspicion is strengthened when we remember that John is well aware of eucharistic practice and language (John 6); it is only natural for him to use eucharistic overtones in his treatment of the Last Supper.

Whether one accepts such a hypothesis or not, there is much in this prayer to provoke thought, even to crown with understanding what has gone in the gospel before. And even after the prayer has been examined, the first thing that seems to strike the reader at first exposure will be the outstanding thing still at the end of the process: the fact that Jesus implored the Father that his disciples be gathered into unity, a prayer that only Christ's disciples can allow to be granted.

MATERIAL

John 17

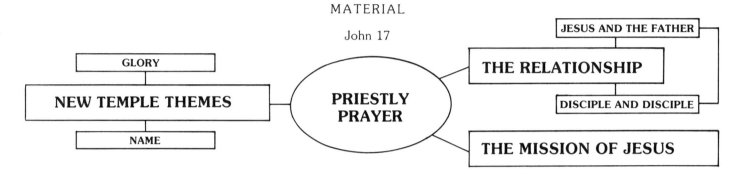

AIM OF SESSION

To complete the Last Supper discourses in the Fourth Gospel with an investigation of the prayer which ends them and its themes.

SESSION NOTES

The Priestly Prayer

— the context of this prayer is obviously at the Last Supper and, in fact, presents us with a closing scene

— if the Fourth Gospel gives a special emphasis to the last discourses of Jesus, the emphasis is even greater to this last extended saying of Christ's in the presence of his disciples

— although spoken in the presence of his followers, this chapter is not addressed to them, but to the Father; it is a glimpse into the type of prayer which Jesus offered during his periods of prayer mentioned so often in the gospels

Given in a context of "plain speaking", Jn 17 elucidates much of the meaning of the death of Jesus:

— the hour of the Cross is the hour of glory (17:1);

— as a result, Jesus will be the bearer of eternal life to his followers (17:2);

— Christ's death will bring him back to the Father as he was with him before (17:11).

Many of the main themes of Jn 17 bring to a climax ideas already familiar to us in the Fourth Gospel:

— the New Temple terms of glory and Name are used repeatedly

— the mission of Jesus is re-emphasised and extended to the mission by Jesus of the disciples

— the relationship between Jesus and the Father is now the basis of unity among the disciples themselves, a fitting conclusion for all the Last Supper teaching on discipleship

John 17 and Eucharist

— it is often noted that John's Gospel contains no institution narrative of the Eucharist; yet in other places he is not negligent about the Eucharist (as in Jn 6 or Jn 15)

— there is a possibility that Jn 17 is related to the very early practice of the Church's prayer at the Eucharist

— the Table Prayer of the *Didachē* uses many of the same central words and ideas (glory, Name, unity, revelation)

— another early source also has tangents of vocabulary and ideas (the second century apocryphal Acts of John uses glory, Name, only God, and world in a sample Eucharistic Prayer)

— perhaps John intends to capture the atmosphere of how the Church prays at the Eucharist in his own description of the Last Supper Prayer.

NOTES ON THE TEXT

17:1 The Johannine emphasis on "the hour" — one of the most characteristic pieces of John's vocabulary — is also attested in Mk 14:41. The close relationship of Father and Son can be seen in their mutual glorification.

17:3 It has been suggested that this verse is a parenthetical remark which was not intended to be read as part of the prayer of Jesus. Certainly the Fourth Gospel seems to have a few instances of such remarks which might be mistaken for quotations (as in Jn 3:16-21 and Jn 3:31-36).

17:5 The pre-existence of Christ, always close to the surface of the Fourth Gospel, shows itself explicitly; the coming events would restore Christ to the glory which he always had with the Father.

17:6 The Name is so much richer a concept in biblical thinking than in modern thought. It contained something special of the person, and for that reason was often used like "glory" to speak of God's presence with his people in the Temple.

17:6-16 The disciples have the word of Jesus in their possession. Their relationship with Jesus makes them distinct from that death-bound human-made system which rejects Jesus, the system which John calls "the world". While distinct from that system, they must live and work surrounded by it; but their attachment to Jesus means that the system which rejected Jesus will hate them, too.

17:17 The disciples are consecrated, or made holy and set apart, by the truth, the truth which is the revelation that Jesus has given them.

17:18-19 Like a High Priest about to offer solemn sacrifice, Jesus consecrates himself on behalf of those for whom he offers. In the Temple worship on the Day of Atonement, the High Priest would first make a sin offering for himself and then for the people; the High Priest of the New Testament makes his sacrifice totally for us.

17:19-23 The famous prayer for unity is explicitly for the generations of Christians descended from the preaching of the disciples. The unity is meant to be as binding as the unity of Father and Son, and grounded in that unity. It is also to be the proof to the world that the mission and message of Jesus is authentic, and a proof of the Father's love for his disciples. There is a lovely phrase in 17:23: *hina ōsin teteleiōmenoi eis hen*, "Let them be perfected/completed into one." We are not the complete disciples that Jesus asks for until we have unity among ourselves; the closer we are to true discipleship, the closer we will be to being one. Reading the New Testament forces one to the opinion that the unity of the Church is as central a teaching as the divinity of Christ.

17:24-26 The disciples who now see Jesus as servant will someday see him in his true glory. But, for the present, the Name of the Father, who is unknown to the world men have made, is revealed to them and the Father's love and Jesus' presence will be with them.

QUESTIONS FOR DISCUSSION

MATERIAL AND DISCUSSION QUESTIONS
FOR SESSION TWENTY-ONE

— This chapter has been styled the priestly prayer of Christ for his Church; what does Christ ask for his Church?

— How is the body of the disciples linked to intimate relationship of Jesus and the Father?

John 18-19

— The Passion story is full of detail showing that Christ is king and the one in total control, even in this "dark hour". Find some of the pointers which John includes.

— Can you see a connection between Ezek 47:1-12, Jn 2:19-22 and Jn 19:31-35?

The Passion in the Fourth Gospel

John 18-19

The Passion is the only twenty-four hours reported in any detail in all four gospels. We have already seen how important it was in the first century to counter the shamefulness of the cross when proclaiming Christ to the Roman world (in Session Sixteen). Indeed, the cross did prove to be a stumbling block and foolishness to many who heard of it (1 Cor 1:23); but those who accepted Jesus saw behind this superficial appearance to the real mystery of the Cross: it was the greatest display of love and faithfulness ever seen in the history of the world.

Throughout the last few chapters of the Fourth Gospel we have noticed two recurring approaches to the death of Christ. One was especially noticeable in chapter twelve: Jesus is anointed and proclaimed as king in preparation for his death. The gospel will turn our attention again to this side of the Passion, to look at these events as the very happenings which show that Christ's royal nature is not seen in pomp and courtly trappings, but in the giving of his life for his people. The second approach is somewhat similar: it treats the crucifixion as the hour of glory and revelation, the moment when Jesus will be known for what he really is. True, that revelation is only going to be understood in the light of the resurrection and the giving of the Holy Spirit; yet, in that light, the cross remains the clearest statement of what Jesus is, what he came to do, the depth of his love, the completeness of his dedication to the Father's will.

Other themes in John's Passion might be pointed out to the group in this Session. The Fourth Gospel, in common with the other gospels, places particular emphasis on the cross as a fulfilment both of the Old Testament Scriptures and of what Jesus himself foretold. When the gospels point out that Jesus predicted some aspects of his Passion, they are telling us that he is in control: the Passion is not something sprung on Christ like a trap on its unsuspecting victim. Jesus knew what he was walking into, and accepted it freely. Unless this were clear, the gospel perspective on the cross as an act of love could never be perceived; the cross would become just the tragic crushing of another innocent victim by ruthless men.

When the gospels point out that the Old Testament is being fulfilled by the Cross of Christ, they are telling us that this was all part of a long planned course of events, something which God knew would happen and for which he tried to prepare his people even in the Old Testament. As long as we have that misconception of prophecy as looking into the future, the fulfilment of prophecies in this way presents no problem. But when we realise what the prophets were really about, then it can present more of a problem. In fact, the texts which John points out as being fulfilled are mostly taken from outside the books of the prophets! So John himself must have understood something other than "prophecies", too. Perhaps we could approach it in this way. The death of Jesus was a travesty of justice, the rejection of God's plan for his people, the exact type of thing that would make you want to say: "Surely the good God cannot stand by and do nothing while this is happening; surely if this were someone beloved of God this would not take place." Yet the Father did not intervene and wicked men did exactly as they wanted to do. But the use of the Scriptures demonstrates that those closest to God often suffered in much the same way, that his messengers were rejected and abused many times before, that wicked men often did as they pleased, and that such situations were recorded again and again in the Scriptures. Of course, John would see the Passion of Jesus as being the ultimate example of this, and more: every instance in the Old Testament of the righteous suffering is pointing forward to the Cross of Jesus, just as every persecution which the disciples endure points back to it (cf. Jn 15:18-25).

There are many things worthy of note in the Passion of John, which is not a simple straightforward account of Good Friday, but a heavily theologised telling of what is for the author a part of the centre of the history of the world. The Passion is hardly just a story for telling — albeit a story which has gripped the imagination of Western civilisation for centuries — it is a story for pondering and meditation, for mental struggle and emotional interplay; and that is how the Fourth Gospel handles it. Some of John's intricate handling we will examine in the notes on passages within the session notes.

The actual death of Jesus, however, deserves a few remarks here. It begins with 19:28, "After this, Jesus aware that all things were already completed — to let the Scripture be fulfilled — says, 'I thirst.' " Traditionally, we look to the statement of thirst as a fulfilment of the Scripture; but should we? Perhaps this is a preliminary, getting the dry, parched lips and tongue ready for the more important announcement of 19:30, "Then when he took the sour wine, Jesus said, 'It stands completed.' " Or to use the familiar Latin rendition, *consummatum est.* "And bowing his head, he handed over the spirit." This second statement is obviously the more important, and 19:28 could be part of the dramatic build-up to it. In the death on the cross, Jesus has completed the mission which the Father entrusted to him. Even the coming of the Spirit on the disciples is hinted at in typically Johannine fashion by the ambiguous phrase, "He handed over the spirit". Obviously John means to say more than that Jesus died. By his death that second comforter is given by Jesus to his disciples, although that giving is to be completed on the day of resurrection (20:22).

What the Fourth Gospel especially dwells on is the piercing of the side of Jesus and the flow of blood and water that follows. What to us is a rather inconsequential detail is underlined by the author with "And the one who has seen this has given his testimony, and his witness is authentic, and this one knows that he speaks correctly, so that you yourselves may believe" (19:35). We can safely conclude that this event had great significance for the author of the Fourth Gospel. Now all we have to do is to figure out why.

John points us to that underused book of Zechariah, by quoting from Zech 12:10. That verse in its full form has interesting overtones of mourning for an only child, a first-born son. But if we continue reading that section of Zechariah, in Zech 13:1, we find a fountain for the cleansing of sin will be opened up for the royal house and for those living in Jerusalem. Perhaps this is something which the fourth gospel had in mind. And then, further on, we read:

On that day living water shall come out from Jerusalem, half towards the eastern sea and half towards the western sea;
in summer and winter it will be there.
And Yahweh will be the king of all the earth;
on that day Yahweh shall be the only one
and his name the only one. (Zech 14:8-9)

As the reader will appreciate by now, in scriptural study one text often borrows another, for all of this water flowing from Jerusalem leads inevitably back to Ezek 47:1-12. There a great river of water, the symbol of every blessing, streams from the Temple of Ezekiel's vision as a sign that God has taken up residence in the restored sanctuary. In other words, John is here bringing to a climax his picture of Jesus as the New Temple, indeed, as the Temple of Ezekiel's vision. By his death, Jesus has fully become the place of perfect sacrifice and complete worship; it is now in Jesus that God and humanity must meet and through him that prayer is offered and through him that blessings are given. His death has been the consecrating sacrifice which has completed the dedication of this living sanctuary. And the sign that the dedication was now complete, and that the New Temple is now God's chosen sanctuary, is a stream of water — just like Ezekiel (and Zechariah) said that it would be. And John records the sign.

When dealing with such rich theology as we find in the gospel accounts of the Passion, one must never imagine that these accounts are spontaneous re-telling of what people just happen to remember. Don't forget that John insists that the disciples didn't understand anything until later, until after the Resurrection and the coming of the Spirit. These are narratives written after the understanding came, not before. They are loaded with thirty, forty, and more years of thinking and talking and preaching and discussing. All of that is given in a highly compact and carefully tailored narrative — just a few short chapters in a very short book.

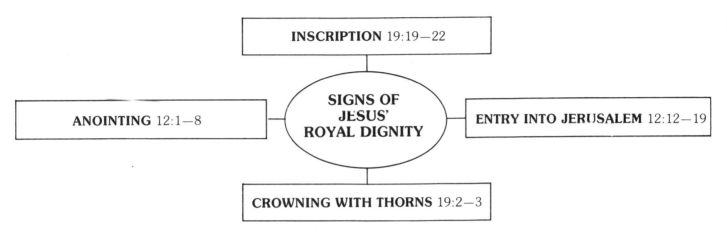

MATERIAL

John 18-19

To examine the studied perspective of the Fourth Gospel on the Passion of Christ; to trace some of the more important themes through the Johannine Passion account.

SESSION NOTES

The Centrality of the Passion

— the Passion and Death give us the only twenty-four hour period reported in any detail in all four gospels

— not only Christ's death, but the shameful way in which it occured was an obstacle to faith in many who heard it (cf. 1 Cor 1:23 and Session Sixteen)

— the narration of the Passion had to be sensitive to the reaction of the audience; yet it does not attempt to deny the apparent shame of the events, only to put a different interpretation on them

— the story of the Passion and Cross is always told as *the* saving event of Christ's life; John particularly views it as the solemn fulfilment of all that Christ came to do

Themes of John's Passion Story

In the Passion, Jesus is most clearly seen as the Royal Messiah; among other signs of his kingly dignity are:

— the anointing at Bethany (Jn 12:1-8);

— the entry into Jerusalem (Jn 12:12-19);

— the crowning with thorns (Jn 19:2-3);

— the inscription on the cross (Jn 19:19-22).

The Hour of the Cross is Jesus' Hour of Glory; it is the moment in which his person and mission can be most clearly seen.

— this clarity of Jesus is matched by the clarity of the rejection of him by the authorities

— it is also the moment when others are seen for their true worth: Peter as a coward, Pilate as an impotent

141

puppet, the Judaeans as God-haters, and Judas as a traitor

— for Jesus, his Hour of Glory will show him to be not only the true King (see above), but also the Paschal Lamb, the New Temple, and the Great "I AM"

The fulfilment of Jesus' word shows that he is in full command of the situation.

— the Cross is not something which takes him by surprise

— he takes the road to Golgotha with perfect freedom

The Old Testament is used by John to show that what is happening is part of God's plan.

— the Old Testament citations are not meant as ancient "prophecies" foretelling the future; most of the direct quotations are not even from the books of the prophets

— the Old Testament is used to show that the suffering of the righteous is not unknown in the ancient Scriptures and that the past suffering now finds its completion in Jesus, just as any hatred of the disciples looks back to the Cross for its meaning

NOTES ON THE TEXT

18:4-6 The passage begins with a note on the foreknowledge of Jesus, a reminder to the reader that he is entering freely into his trial and execution. But why does the arresting party fall down when Jesus answers them? The answer is significant for interpreting some of the central sayings of the fourth gospel. When Jesus says, "I am he", he is using the words *ego eimi*, so often used before in the gospel (especially in the *I am* sayings);

by falling to the ground, the chief priests and Pharisees are acknowledging *ego eimi* as the divine name (cf. Ex 3:12-14), thus telling us something about the other uses of that phrase in the Fourth Gospel

18:8-9 Again, Christ in control. He tells the mob who to arrest and who not to arrest, and his saying is fulfilled. His free choice is again emphasised by the statement to Peter in 18:11.

18:16 This verse would seem to indicate that the authority behind the Fourth Gospel was known to the Jerusalem authorities — an interesting aside which could lend great authenticity to sections such as 11:45-53.

18:17-26 John, like Mark, splits the triple denial of Peter to frame the open testimony of Jesus before the religious authority.

18.31-32 The exact extent of Jewish authority to execute criminals is not clear; the evidence shows that executions did occur. However, only Romans crucified, and John is showing us that only crucifixion would fulfil what Jesus said about his death being a lifting up or exaltation (Jn 3:14; 8:28; 12:32-33); Jesus' foreknowledge demonstrates his freedom and control.

18:33-39 The pivot of the trial before Pilate is the title "King of the Jews". The very term seems to be a foreigner's corruption of the more Hebrew "King of Israel" (e.g. Jn 12:13) and should be more exactly translated "King of the Judaeans". Interestingly enough Pilate is not informed of any charge against Jesus, yet automatically interrogates him about his supposed kingship, which prompts Jesus' reply: "Are you saying this from yourself or did others say this about me?"

19:2-3 The Roman soldiers crown and salute Jesus, albeit in mockery. Even the purple garment had royal connotations. For John, this is a real coronation; perhaps the irony is even deeper since the kings and tetrarchs of the period received their appointment from the Roman authorities. Jesus, too, is acknowledged as "King of the Judaeans" by the Romans.

19:9 Pilate asks the crucial question, "Where do you come from?" If he could accept the answer, then he would accept the whole mystery of salvation which Jesus brought.

19:11 Here is another play with the word *anōthen*, here meaning "from above". When Pilate hears that his authority is given from above, he undoubtedly thinks of Rome; What Jesus means is that his authority is allowed him from God, or else none of this would be taking place.

19:14 The time marker here reminds the reader that Jesus is brought to Golgotha during the time that the lambs were being sacrificed for the Passover meal.

19:14-15 The Judaeans, when presented with their promised King, ironically choose their oppressors, the Roman Emperor and his troops.

19:19-22 Part of the ancient royal inauguration was the public proclamation that the king's rule had begun; the title on the cross, in the three official languages, in a public place is meant to be the proclamation of Christ's reign.

19:24 The psalm which is quoted is Ps 22, well worth a read in light of the Passion. It was also seen as an important text in the synoptic tradition of the story of Good Friday.

19:26-27 Although Acts of the Apostles mentions the Lord's mother among the disciples at prayer, this short passage is the sole evidence that Mary took part in the great drama of the

Passion. The term "woman" (Greek: *gunē*) is again used where we would expect to find "mother"; perhaps it was a type of pet name which Jesus had for Mary (cf. Jn 2:4). It might also be noted that in both cases in the Fourth Gospel where the mother of Christ is mentioned, it is in the context of disciples being present.

19:28-29 Although the concern of Jesus to fulfil the Scriptures is often linked with "I thirst", it is also possible that Jesus is preparing his parched lips for the solemn statement of verse thirty. If the statement of thirst is itself meant to fulfil the Scripture, then the most likely candidate is again Ps 22 (verse fifteen).

19:30 The death of Jesus completes what he has come to do, thus fulfilling not just one particular passage of Scripture, but the entire Old Testament. The second part of the verse speaks of the handing over of the Spirit by Christ – certainly meant to say that Jesus died, but also meant to hint at the great gift brought by his death.

19:31-37 The piercing of Jesus' side is the high point of John's account of the death of Christ. Perhaps John has in mind prophetic texts concerned with the renewed Temple from which a fountain would spring, thus bringing to a high point his image of Jesus as the New Temple, the new place of worship and sacrifice, the new meeting place of God and humanity. Those prophecies would include Zech 12:10; 13:1; 14:8-9; Ezek 47:1-12.

19:38-41 All of the gospels place a certain importance on the burial. Culturally, the burial was an irrefutable statement of death (which is perhaps why it appears in the verbally economic Apostles' Creed). The announcement of the Resurrection also demands that the exact location of the place of burial was noted and remembered; otherwise mention of an empty tomb would be meaningless.

QUESTIONS FOR DISCUSSION

— The Passion story is full of detail showing that Christ is king and the one in total control, even in this "dark hour". Find some of the pointers which John includes.

— Can you see a connection between Ezek 47:1-12, Jn 2:19-22 and John 19:31-35?

MATERIAL AND DISCUSSION QUESTIONS
FOR SESSION TWENTY-TWO

John 20-21

— Why is the story of Thomas included? It comes at the very end of what most scholars feel is the first edition of the Fourth Gospel.

— Does Jn 21:24-25 tell you something about the composition of the Fourth Gospel?

The Resurrection

John 20-21

The way in which we treat the gospel accounts of the Resurrection, both in the liturgy and in humbler approaches such as Bible study sessions, can give a very false impression — that Good Friday and Easter Sunday are nearly non-connected. We cut a deep divide between texts which are united in the New Testament; even the relatively modern chapter divisions might divert our attention from the natural unity which flows from the trial to the death to the burial to the resurrection of Jesus. It is all part of one story, a story with an unpredictable twist to be sure, but one connected story all the same.

No other place in the gospel narratives is so central to our belief as Christians as this story of Good Friday and Easter Sunday. On the whole, the gospels are not overly concerned with history in the way that we are. The earliest witness which we have to the writing of the gospels even mentions that Mark was not particularly anxious about chronological order. But when we enter the last acts of the story of Jesus, history becomes more and more important. For the apostles and evangelists, the resurrection of Jesus was not just a romantic expression of how truth will never die ("The message of Jesus lives on") nor an observation that what Christ tried to do will be continued in them ("Jesus lives on in his followers"). The Resurrection was a cold fact, one that turned over their whole logic about life and death, one for which most of them were to give their lives. Paul made the classic statement about the historicity of the resurrection: "If Christ has not been raised, then empty is our preaching, empty too your faith... If we have hoped in Christ as far as this life alone is concerned, then we are more to be pitied than everyone else" (I Cor 15:14,19).

Yet it is not enough simply to re-assert the historical truth of the resurrection. Certainly to find that Jesus was alive when his followers presumed him dead is wonderful in itself — but it only scratches the surface of the biblical truth. Resurrection is not just a coming back to life again. Even a quick read of I Cor 15 should be enough to show that we are talking about a totally different kind of life, a totally different kind of body. Paul uses the image of a seed going into the ground and a plant which looks quite different coming up: more alive, flourishing, giving life (I Cor 15:35-44). The Fourth Gospel uses the same image to speak of the death (and resurrection) of Jesus in Jn 12:23-25. The example was obviously an appropriate one for showing that for the one person there can be dramatically different modes of being alive. And the resurrection life is always looked upon as being the greater and fuller — in marked contrast to, say, the Egyptian view of life after death or even to the sophistic attempts to restate the resurrection in terms which do not imply a physical rising.

Set the Easter story against the Jewish belief of the time concerning the resurrection and another aspect emerges. Of course, not all Jews believed in a resurrection (cf. Mk 12:18-25), but some did. Their belief is summarised by Dan 12:1-3 — the resurrection of the just would be the final act in salvation history, God's greatest and final deed on behalf of his people. When Jesus is raised (and the New Testament often speaks of him being raised by the Father rather than rising because of his own divine power), it is a statement by the Father that all that Jesus said and did was acceptable to him, the ultimate vindication of the person and ministry of Christ. And the early Church also recognised that the final act had begun, that we are now in the last days of history. Reading I Cor 15:20-24 or Peter's speech in Acts 2:14-36 should be proof enough of that.

Whenever we speak of the resurrection of Jesus, then, three aspects of its scriptural message should be kept to the fore: the resurrection of Jesus is *not* a philosophical statement, but a physical happening which occured in time and space; resurrection is not just coming back to life, but coming to a new type of life with a new type of bodily existence; the resurrection of Jesus is the first act in the resurrection of the dead and the beginning of the last stage in history. It should be evident from the last two statements that the resurrection of Lazarus (or of the daughter of Jairus or of the son of the widow of Nain) was not a resurrection in the same sense: these people all died again. They experienced resuscitation, Jesus was the first to experience resurrection.

John's particular treatment of the resurrection is contained in chapter twenty of the Fourth Gospel, which breaks very naturally into three sections. The first section is the discovery, basically there to tell the story of the empty tomb. The second section is the appearance of Jesus to his disciples and the giving of the Spirit. The third section is the famous episode of "Doubting Thomas" which finishes with these verses:

> Many were the other signs which Jesus did in front of his disciples, signs which are not written in this book. These ones are written so that you might believe that Jesus is the Messiah, the Son of God, and so that when you believe you might have life in his name (Jn 20:30-31).

Clearly, an earlier edition of the Fourth Gospel ended here. The impact was a suitable conclusion: you, the reader, are like Thomas — you have not seen the risen Jesus; you did not even see him in his earthly ministry. Will you be like Thomas in not accepting the word of those who have seen him, or will you believe and let the blessing of Christ for those who have not seen and yet believe fall upon you?

The gospel which we hold in our hands, however, does not end with chapter twenty. There is another chapter which is no less Scripture than any other part of the Fourth Gospel; yet, because it is added after the natural conclusion, it is usually referred to as the "epilogue". It has some very attractive material in it, but seems to be more concerned with the disciples after the resurrection than with the meaning of the resurrection. The epilogue begins with a fishing scene, moves into a resurrection appearance, and then has a dialogue with Simon Peter. The dialogue with Simon Peter concludes with a reference to the beloved disciple which has these verses at the end:

> This is the disciple who testifies about these things and who wrote them, and we know that his testimony is true. There are many other things which Jesus did. If they were each written down, I don't suppose that the world itself would hold the books that could be written (Jn 21:24-25).

This would seem to be the verification of the disciple's testimony by someone other than the disciple — probably the editor of the book as we have it. One reason that the epilogue might be included is this: the disciple had lived for a long time, outliving even Peter's martyrdom. A rumour was circulating that this disciple was promised to be alive at the time of the second coming. But this disciple, too, had died, causing some unnecessary consternation. The one who handed on his tradition wanted to make it quite clear that there had never been any promise that he would live to the second coming, and so this epilogue was written. Such a theory is close to the evidence as we have it in Jn 21:20-23.

Because we are by nature curious creatures, a session on the Resurrection is bound to raise many questions. John's theology of the Resurrection would never claim to be the complete treatment of the subject in the New Testament, and certainly is not a systematic treatment. The leader of the group would be well advised to take a close look at I Cor 15 where Paul tries to answer some questions which arose about the Resurrection in his own day. Ultimately, however, we must admit that the resurrection is something promised to us but yet not experienced by us. When we experience it, then our questions will be answered.

Biblical resurrection is quite different from other ancient ideas of the afterlife.

MATERIAL

Jn 20-21

AIM OF SESSION

To gain some insight into the New Testament treatment of the resurrection of Jesus; to look at the account of the resurrection experience in the Fourth Gospel.

SESSION NOTES

The Resurrection in the New Testament

No event in the New Testament is more central to Christian belief than the death and resurrection of Jesus.

— the two should be seen as a united event; all accounts of the Passion are interwoven with an account of the discovery of the empty tomb

— it is central that the resurrection is seen as an historical happening

— it is not a romantic insight that Jesus lives on in his followers or in his teaching

— although undoubtedly of a new order of reality, the resurrection of Jesus has a physical aspect

— the importance of its historical truth does not rule out differences in the telling of the story of Easter; the four gospels all have differing details in the story of the discovery of the tomb and different resurrection appearances

The resurrection is not just a coming back to life; it is a new type of life and a new type of bodily existence.

— the classic expression of this difference is given by Paul in 1 Cor 15:35-44; this body compared to the resurrection body is like a seed compared to the full-grown plant

The resurrection of Jesus would have signified to the disciples that a new stage in God's plan had been reached; the resurrection at the end of time had been begun, and humanity is now in its last days.

— the resurrection hope contained in a passage such as Dan 12:1-3 was seen to be the final act of God on behalf of his people

— in this context, it should be noted that usually the New Testament speaks of Jesus "being raised" by the Father

— it is a mark of approval by the Father on all that Jesus said and did, a complete vindication from the capital charge of blasphemy

— the New Testament also acknowledges that the divine Son had the ability and power to rise from death (Jn 10:17-18)

— the New Testament preaching of the resurrection was not to prove Christ's divinity, but to prove that he was God's Messiah (Acts 2:22-36)

The Resurrection in the Fourth Gospel

The basic treatment of the resurrection is to be found in John chapter twenty, which has three parts.

The first part is the discovery of the empty tomb (20:1-18)

— in common with other narrations of this discovery is the complete surprise which the disciples show: life has continued as normal — no one expected a resurrection

— as in the other three gospels, Mary Magdalene is mentioned, but no mention is made of any companions

— the lack of understanding which has shown itself here and there in the gospel begins to dissipate with the sight of the empty tomb (20:8-9)

The second part is the appearance of the risen Christ to the disciples.

— this contains John's account of the giving of the Spirit, a different picture from the Pentecost of Acts, but the same theological reality

The third part is "Doubting Thomas" and the conclusion of the earlier edition (20:30-31).

— the reader is in a similar position to Thomas's; having heard the testimony of others, the reader must decide whether to accept it or not

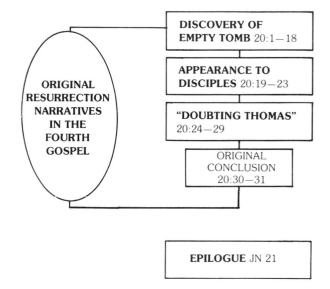

20:1-3 Unlike the synoptic accounts, there is no messenger in John to explain the meaning of the empty tomb — in fact, the emptiness is misconstrued as a removal of the corpse. The disciples are also brought in at a much earlier stage. Resurrection is far from anyone's mind.

20:8-9 The faith referred to here is embryonic: the penny is only beginning to drop for John.

20:12 The angelic messengers are introduced, yet their message is not the full announcement of the resurrection as in the synoptics.

20:15-16 The misunderstanding of Mary has just the gentlest touch of John's humour, underscoring the ridiculous contrast of Mary's grief and torment on the day of her greatest joy.

20:17 Much ink has been spilt over the first words of Christ's statement. The Greek implies that Mary is already touching Jesus, either holding him — or perhaps clasping at him to make certain that he's real.

20:19 C.S. Lewis pointed out that Jesus did not walk through walls and doors because he was more ethereal, as if he were a ghost, but because he was more solid than door and walls, as with us when we walk through air and fog. Whatever about his physics, Lewis captured the theological flavour of the image. The peace greeting is the normal Jewish "Shalom", which receives its fullest meaning in this context of Easter reunion.

20:21-22 The relationship between Jesus and his disciples is now analogous to the relationship of Jesus during his mission to his Father. The promised Holy Spirit is given, with authority over sin.

20:25 If nothing else, Thomas's refusal to believe shows just how physically the New Testament understands resurrection; while physical, it is certainly wider than the reality which we now know.

20:28-29 The confession of faith is an unequivocal statement of the divinity of Jesus. It may be meant to close the book on the same note on which it began (cf. Jn 1:1). The blessing is not meant for Thomas but for the reader.

20:30-31 This conclusion is fairly decisive evidence that an earlier edition of the gospel ended here. It also points to the fact that gospels were not written as disinterested journalism, but as documents to bring faith. This ending also gives the impression that it is written as much for the non-believer as the believer, although no firm conclusion could be drawn from it.

The Epilogue

Although an early edition of the Fourth Gospel seems to have ended with 20:31, there is an additional chapter in the gospel as we have it; because it is after the main body of the gospel, it is often called the "epilogue".

— the concluding verses would point to this inclusion by a later editor, himself a follower of the disciple, who can stand behind the authenticity of the disciple's testimony

The epilogue begins with a fishing scene, not a familiar one from the Fourth Gospel, but the epilogue presumes that such scenes are associated by the reader with Jesus and the disciples.

— there is some question of the identity of the Lord (cf. 21:12); such non-recognition throughout the gospel accounts of the resurrection appearances are a good indication that the bodily form of Jesus had changed

Peter has a prominent place in the epilogue:

— he is asked specifically about his love for the Lord

— to Peter is committed the task of shepherding

— his role is based clearly in his relationship to Jesus, just as in Mt 16 it is based on his profession of faith

The Disciple, too, has a special place; it may be because of him that the epilogue is included.

— the epilogue may be written to refute the rumour that Jesus had promised the Disciple that he would be left until the second coming

— such a rumour would especially to be a problem if, in fact, the Disciple had recently died; the epilogue would show that the death of the Disciple was not in contradiction to the Lord's promise

21:1 The synoptic tradition of the resurrection has two different places for the resurrection appearances to the disciples: Luke says that Jerusalem was the location, Matthew and Mark hold for Galilee. The Fourth Gospel in its present state seems to allow for both: the appearances of chapter twenty in Jerusalem and the appearance in the epilogue in Galilee.

21:5-6 This presumes that a tradition of an earlier miraculous catch of fish (such as in Lk 5:1-11) is familiar to the audience, even though no such miracle is recounted in the Fourth Gospel. It is an indication that the Fourth Gospel received its final form after the other gospels were in circulation.

21:11 Of the many interpretations offered for the one hundred and fifty three fish, Augustine's is most appealing. He says that there are supposedly one hundred and fifty three species of fish in the world, and that the catch is meant to show the disciples that all sorts and types of humanity were to be gathered into the nets of the Church by the fishers of men. The unbroken nets would then mean that the Church should be wide enough and universal enough to accept all who are drawn to Jesus.

21:13 Eating with the risen Lord is sometimes meant to be reminiscent of the Eucharist, as in Lk 24:28-35. Such an implication here would tie in well with the ecclesial interpretation of the fish and net in 21:11.

21:15-17 The dialogue between Peter and Jesus depends on a difference of words in the Greek, *agapaō* (meaning concern and care, the normal New Testament type of love) and *phileō* (meaning to be fond of someone, to be a friend — not as lofty a type of love as *agapaō*). In the first two questions Jesus uses *agapeō*, "Peter, do you care about me more than these?", and Peter answers with *phileō*, "Yes, Lord, you know that I'm fond of you." the third time Jesus asks the question with *phileō*, which is often seen as Christ coming down to Peter's level. The shepherding of the flock is especially entrusted to Peter.

21:18-19 Peter's later execution is part of his following of Christ, which began at the Sea of Galilee.

21:20-23 This may be the reason for the inclusion of the epilogue: some people were saying that the Disciple would never die, and the author of the epilogue wanted to make it clear that this was a misinterpretation of what was said.

21:24-25 This is a second conclusion to the Fourth Gospel, and it is written by someone who vouches for the authenticity of the Disciple's witness.

QUESTIONS FOR DISCUSSION

— Why is the story of Thomas included? It comes at the very end of what most scholars feel is the first edition of the Fourth Gospel.

— Does Jn 21:24-25 tell you something about the composition of the Fourth Gospel?

— What is the future of this group?

Notes

Notes